*Jordana—*

# HILDA

TACKLE YOUR INNER NAYSAYER,
GET OUT OF YOUR OWN WAY,
AND UNLEASH YOUR BADASSERY

*It's Your Turn!*

Jennie Mustafa-Julock

*Wishing you + your gorgeous family every sweet imagined possibility!*

*P.S. I'd love to hear what you think about my book!*

HILDA: Tackle Your Inner Naysayer, Get Out of Your Own Way, and Unleash Your Badassery

Coach Jennie
The Audacity Coach
www.coachjennie.com/contact

Illustrations: Renee Bates
Cover Design: Megan Atkinson

First Edition

Hilda by Jennie Mustafa-Julock
ISBN 978-0-9979838-0-7

# Contents

*Dedicated to Meredyth*

*The only person on the planet who is strong enough to put up with me and my Hilda.*

*If you're reading this book, you aim to lead a life that matters.*

*I totally love that about you.*

*The following is a book about self-sabotage.*

# A Letter from Hilda

I cannot believe you are reading this book right now. I did everything I could possibly think of to derail Jennie from writing this book. Seriously. Everything imaginable.

I told her that she didn't know what she was talking about.

I repeatedly drilled into her head that she didn't have enough to fill an entire book.

I distracted her with shiny objects, like the time I encouraged her to do hours of online shopping for the perfect pocketbook that she never bought.

I convinced her to only consider traditional publishing because I knew that her fear of rejection would keep her from ever submitting a book proposal. That one worked for almost a year.

I reminded her that self-published authors never make any real impact and that she didn't have what it takes to be one of those stand-out indie publishers who makes it big.

I interrupted every writing session with copious amounts of self-doubt. I convinced her that she was a shitty writer. That writing a book would be too hard. And even harder for her than anyone else. Obviously.

I served as her co-conspirator in self-sabotage daily. Like the time we binged on 19 episodes of Game of Thrones in one weekend. Impossible to write when the laptop is occupied with HBONOW.

I made her believe she was too busy and too basic to write a decent book. Who does she think she is? Tony Robbins? Oprah? Please.

And it worked like a charm . . . for a while. But somehow she pressed on despite all of my painstaking efforts to keep her from putting herself out there. To keep her safe.

Whatever.

She doesn't listen. It's infuriating. But whatever.

So here you go. A book about me.

Not like it's gonna help anyway.

# Meet Coach Jennie

Before you dive into this book, I bet you'd like to know a bit about who I am. My name is Jennie Mustafa-Julock, The Audacity Coach (yep, the "The" is purposely capitalized). Everyone just calls me Coach Jennie. In 2006, I hung out my shingle with that confident title and I have built my life and business coaching practice around it. I specialize in helping ambitious badasses who are on the brink of something spectacular figure out *how* to make it happen.

The word *how* in that pithy little elevator pitch is extremely loaded. While much of the work I do with clients involves crafting a vision for their spectacular dream and developing a smart strategy for making it happen, that's honestly only part of the *how*. The rest of the *how* is in dealing with their self-sabotage. Every. single. client. Not one of them has been immune to the Hilda.

I'm an expert in self-sabotage, inside and out, whether I intended to be or not. I have worked with hundreds of people on figuring out why and how they sabotage themselves and co-creating ways to change it. I also bring an enormous amount of expertise on self-sabotage from being a master in holding myself back. Allow me to elaborate.

## Picture this: Boston, 2006

Thirty years old and happily married. Well, not *legally married* quite yet, but times they were a-changing. I was an intensely ambitious young woman hellbent on making a difference, dare I say, changing the world in some way.

I had bootstrapped myself out of poverty - the first person in my family to go to college, let alone graduate school - to become successful with my fancy-pants degrees and my fancy-pants job as an organizational development consultant for government organizations. I had worked my ass off to achieve this status and I was damn proud of what I had accomplished.

But I was unbearably miserable.

And then I got laid off.

I decided to start my own coaching practice.

Immediately after I proclaimed to my wife *I am going to become a life coach,* I started hearing my inner naysayer's voice:

> *Who do you think you are?*
> *You don't know what you're talking about.*
> *Who on earth is gonna want to listen to your advice?*
> *You're woefully unqualified to call yourself a coach.*
> *You think someone is going to actually PAY you to help them?*
> *They'll find out you're a phony.*
> *I mean, what will your dad think?*
> *This isn't realistic, Jennie.*
> *You're too young.*

*and too fat*
*and too gay*
*and too this*
*and too that.*
*Face it: you're going to fail!*

Yep. That sounds like my Hilda alright. More on her in due time.

You know this story. Every entrepreneur and visionary and badass in general I know has some version of it. You decide to take a leap, start your side hustle, launch a solo venture, write a book, whatever because you know that life has to be more than just punching a clock and blah, blah, blah. But rarely do we look inside the brains of these stories. Until now, that is.

## What Can You Expect from Me?

You'll also quickly learn I'm not like most of the life coaches you've come across. I don't subscribe to the gentle encouragement coaching thing. My signature cathartic shoves get you unstuck and make you unstoppable. My BS-free approach to so-much-more-than-life coaching has been the catalyst for my clients to launch new businesses, publish their first books, negotiate career leaps, adventure the world, and more. Simply put, I help driven individuals on the brink of something badass bust through obstacles and build the audacious lives they've been dreaming about. And you can expect that kind of experience with this book, too.

## Oh, the Audacity! Wait, huh?

I'm the poster-child of audacity! Since birth, I've challenged the world around me: I refuse to color within the lines, stay inside the box, or play by the rules. Instead, I'm driven to craft a career and life that suits me and only ME! And I do so in a way that not only leaves room for others to prosper alongside me, but encourages them to do so.

Basically, I aim to make a big, badass splash in everything I do. My Audacity Coaching practice and community, in its tenth year as of the publication of this book, has helped some of the most brilliant, ambitious professionals around catapult their lives into the next level of awesomeness - I call this living audaciously.

It's a mission of mine to shatter the status quo that life coaching has to be a spiritual, warm and fuzzy, woo-woo experience where you are coddled endlessly and given platitudes that make you feel good but take you nowhere. This gives the title of "Coach" a bad rap and that breaks my heart. It's time to redefine the reputation of what great coaching can be – a swift kick in the ass so you realize much more potential, do extraordinary things with your time and energy, and be the best damn version of yourself possible.

## It's time to live audaciously!

*I am on a mission to instigate audacity in as many humans as possible . . .*

*. . . and then watch the world change.*

# Cue the Vulnerability

I need to make a confession. I really, reallllly didn't want to write this book.

As much as I enjoy talking about Hilda, I didn't want to be known as an authority on the inner critic and self-sabotage. It felt too negative or something. I wanted to be known for the big, beautiful, bold, super positive concept of audacity!

I didn't want to write a book on self-sabotage. I just didn't. I fought the idea of writing this book tooth and nail. When my team came to me and said, "Coach Jennie, we know you want to write a book about goal setting. We know you want to write a book on your signature Confidence Continuum™, but the book we really want is one about Hilda!" I told them they were crazy. I even laughed at them. I'm The Audacity Coach! I want to be known as somebody that helps people tap into their audacity, so that they can do whatever spectacular thing they are meant to do in this world. That's what I DO. And I LOVE the idea of Hilda, right? I created it. I'm a big fan - obviously! But to be known as the Hilda coach? That's not what I wanted. That's not what I signed up for. I want to be known for audacity - not Hilda!!

On top of that, the concept of the inner critic is simply not original. Far from it. There are countless articles, research papers, books, therapists, authors, coaches, and other assorted resources dedicated to the topic of self-sabotage. So I constantly question the wisdom of writing about it yet again. Does the world really need yet another book on the inner critic? Well, maybe not. Maybe the world will be just fine if I keep my spin on the inner saboteur tucked away in my small, but mighty coaching community.

Eventually, I had to listen. I mean they brought it up more than once. They brought it up individually. They brought it up together. My wife brought it up. Pretty much everyone who has ever met Hilda has asked me, "When are you going to write a book about that?" Years later, I've come to realize and accept that self-sabotage is a universal experience and tackling it through the lens of Hilda makes it almost universally relatable.

So here we are. Hilda, the book.

But getting here wasn't easy.

Because admitting I'm the expert on self-sabotage, even though the topic fascinates me beyond measure when it comes to other people, included having to deal with my own self-sabotage. Damn, I was not ready for that! You see, I am the queen of self-sabotage. I am ridiculously good at it. I even sabotage myself, while sabotaging myself.

I'm the kind of person that when I feel bad, I feel bad about feeling bad, because I shouldn't be worthy of such feelings. So now I will beat myself up about the fact that I feel bad. I'm the person ordering a pizza while watching the Biggest Loser and simultaneously wishing my jeans fit better. (True story. Don't judge me.)

I self-sabotage in a big, big way and as I started writing this book, my self-sabotage surprisingly got worse! I was suddenly uber-aware of every time I screwed myself over, procrastinated, changed my mind, obsessed about what someone else thought, or hit a drive-thru for dinner.

Every twist, turn, and tango with Hilda shared in this book is one I've experienced first-hand. Sure, most of the stories I share are those of my clients . . . and the specifics of their stories are theirs. Deeply, personally, and exclusively theirs (and, of course, only shared here with their permission). I may not have fought the very same battles, but I've been in the same trenches with Hilda.

I've had the same feelings of inadequacy and self-doubt. I've convinced myself of my imminent failure and impending doom. I've run screaming from enormous opportunities because I didn't want others to think poorly of me. And so on and so on.

I, myself, am an expert orchestrator of self-sabotage in my own life (as I'm sure you are, too).

With that being said, this book is not a memoir. It's not a recollection of my struggles with Hilda.

And this book is not a manifesto. It's not stuffed cover-to-cover with words to live by and rules to abide by.

This book is a carefully-woven, meticulously-crafted, and painstakingly-honest collection of truths. Written by me, but co-created through hundreds and hundreds of hours of honesty and vulnerability with clients, friends, family, and even complete strangers.

I'm going to teach you about the four different ways I've seen Hilda show up. And I want to delight you. I want to make sure that this is an enjoyable journey for you. In my coaching practice one of our ground rules is, "If we're not having fun, we're doing it wrong," so if you're not having fun with this book at any point, skip ahead, jump around, go to a different section that feels more relevant.

I want you to love this book because of its impact. I want it to be more than another one of those self-help books that give you a lot of rah-rah-rah-sis-boom-bah-kum-ba-ya BS, but never actually amounts to much. I want this to *work* for you.

And I trust that it will - despite my own Hilda trying to convince me otherwise while I write these very words.

The foundation from which this book was built upon is constructed of hundreds upon hundreds upon hundreds of hours of client sessions, stories from friends and family, conversations within my community, and some pretty ridiculously hardcore research on my part.

It's backed up by science, by other researchers and experts, and by my own personal experiences too.

It's legit, Hilda. OK? Get off my back.

This material is battle-tested and skeptic-approved. And I'm just dying for you to dive in.

This is not just 'yet another' self-help book on self-sabotage and the inner critic.

No.

This is my opus.

Thank you for reading.

# CHAPTER ONE

# Meet Hilda

S elf-sabotage is real. Let's say you've decided to start something spectacular. Brilliant! But almost immediately after you proclaim, "I am going to {insert your goal here}" you start hearing her voice . . .

*You're dreaming far too big for someone like you.*
*You know you're going to fail. Why even try?*
*They will find out you're a phony, y'know.*
*Pfffft, this could never happen for you.*
*People are going to laugh at you.*
*Why can't you just be grateful?*
*That's a really, really bad plan.*
*You shouldn't have said that.*
*Who do you think you are?*
*You're not good enough.*
*You don't wanna.*
*You don't know.*
*You shouldn't.*
*You won't.*
*You can't.*
*You suck.*

. . . I know it ain't just me.

You know this voice. You've heard it before. You may even be hearing it right now. And if you're like everyone I have ever met, the voice in your head already has some signature phrases designed to torture you. This voice is upsetting and pervasive.

## I like to call her *Hilda*.

Hilda is the name I give to your irksome, inner naysayer who constantly tells you how much you suck. She's the annoying, internal personal saboteur inside your brain that tells you incessantly that you're not good enough. She jabs you in the ribs when she thinks you're getting too big for your britches. She takes note of all your past failures and sends you not-so-gentle reminders of those moments every time a new idea arises. She's the nagging, negative voice inside your brain that relentlessly picks away at your sense of possibility, your ambitions, your confidence, and your tenacity.

She's the one with the disempowering messages who cunningly chips away at your potential. While you're shaking out dusty beliefs, creating fresh mindsets, and setting new and lofty goals, Hilda's in your head spewing nonsense to trigger self-doubt, self-consciousness, second-guessing, and defeat.

Her sole job in your life is to keep you small. To keep you stuck. To keep you safe.

Because she doesn't want you to get yelled at.

Or get burned.

Or embarrassed.

Or fail miserably.

Or get uncomfy in any way whatsoever.

She LOVES to be comfortable.

And unfortunately, she's really freaking good at getting her way.

Why did I dub my inner critic *Hilda*? Because to me, it was the most ridiculous name I could think of and that instantly ruined her credibility. (Apologies to all who share her name. Feel free to call yours *Jennie*. It's only fair.) Titles like "the inner critic" or worse yet "the inner saboteur" are soft and froo-froo and professional sounding and give her far too much power and credence. Instead, I opt for the absurd.

If she were a Game of Thrones character, she would be addressed as *Hilda: Queen of the House of Self-Sabotage, Keeper of the Status Quo, Enforcer of Mediocrity, Chief Fear Monger, and Curator of Defeatist Thoughts and Feelings.*

This naming ritual separates her *fear-driven, twisted messages* from *my truth*. It allows me to build a virtual wall between what I want and what she wants.

That's just straight up logic, yo.

Just because these messages reside inside of your brain doesn't mean this nonsense is true. It doesn't mean there's something wrong with you either . . . you're perfectly normal. It's just some voice inside your head that's gathered a bunch of information from all of the situations, experiences, and people who have held you back in life and created this cesspool of suckdom in your mind.

# How She Operates

## Why She's Strong

Because you believe her. Because until now, you didn't know all this noise was *her*, not *you*! She lives in your brain, so she must be telling you the truth, right? And because you've proved her right over and over again by following her rules, sabotaging your dreams, and staying small, she's won. Repeatedly. So when she pipes up, your Pavlovian response follows.

## Why She's Wrong

Because you want more. Because you're a badass. Because no matter how much of your confidence she's swallowed up in the past, you can always go out and find more. And because you've got evidence to the contrary of all her silly notions. Others have been able to do what you want to do, so it has been proven possible. Again, logic.

## What She Says

Your Hilda is conniving and knows all the best ways to get under your skin. Hilda's job is to provide false and misleading evidence that these beliefs are founded. She twists your past experiences to reinforce these misguided beliefs. She fills your head with cynical nonsense (your thoughts) to remind you to feel a certain way (your feelings), which then dictates your next move (your actions). When she pulls all those strings just right, the naysaying noise she plants in your brain makes you feel nervous and scared and embarrassed and uncertain and keeps you from taking any action. And when she wins, she smugly kicks, completely satisfied that she's managed to keep you safe and sound – and stuck.

In my inexhaustible obsession to understand Hilda and her self-sabotaging ways, I have surmised that not all Hildas take the same form. But after coaching hundreds of audacious people over the last decade, I've noticed four very specific patterns we humans tend to follow in our adventures with self-sabotage. Or to be more direct, we're all susceptible to Hilda's four BS Beliefs. When you are about to do something that matters, Hilda will convince you of one or more of the following BS Beliefs . . .

## I Can't

*I Can't* Hilda amplifies self-doubt and defeatism. She makes you feel insecure and convinces you to question your capability. She attacks your confidence.

## I Shouldn't

*I Shouldn't* Hilda obsesses about the judgments of others. She makes you feel judged and convinces you to change your behavior to please other people. She attacks your possibilities.

## I Don't Know

*I Don't Know* Hilda perpetuates inertia and indecision for as long as humanly possible. She makes you feel stuck and convinces you to second guess your every desire. She attacks your ambition.

## I Don't Wanna

*I Don't Wanna* Hilda justifies inaction and procrastination. She makes you feel unfocused and convinces you to avoid your goals. She attacks your tenacity.

The first two BS Beliefs strike at the heart of who you are. The second two combat the core of what you want.

Ambitious people are almost always hearing nonsense from at least one of these Hildas. Some even manage to tolerate duets, trios, and even quartets of naysaying BS in unison.

# Demented Documentarian

Hilda loves your personal history. She hangs out in your brain filming every moment of your life. Every time you do anything that matters to you, she busts out her camera and captures every memory and emotion that goes along with it. She carefully files each of these experiences and memories away.

But like most documentary filmmakers, Hilda has a particular bias that is infused in your story. Seriously, Michael Moore and Morgan Spurlock got nothing on Hilda. She cuts and slices and amplifies the moments where you are at your worst. Whenever you're about to do something that makes her the least bit uncomfortable, she sets up a screening of your mental documentary to scare the crap out of you.

If you've ever had a moment where you've backed down, oh she knows the transcript of that moment. If you've ever failed and landed dramatically on your ass, yep she knows that play-by-play too.

> *Hey. Remember this time when you embarrassed the crap out yourself? Yeah, that's what this choice will do.*

> *Hey. Remember how bad this moment was? No? Allow me to revisit it and make you feel like that again.*

> *Hey. Remember what your mother used to say to keep you from making a mistake? I'm just gonna put that track on a loop so you hear it over and over and over again, in your mother's voice no less, to remind you to behave yourself and not upset your dead mother.*

## Enough already!

Hilda shows up for your most triumphant moments, too. She just hides those archives away in the deep recesses of your mind, often downplaying their significance. Sometimes, she even makes you feel bad for having a sense of pride, lest you get too big for your britches.

# But Hilda Means Well

*Wait, what now?*

Believe it or not, Hilda means well. She's as mean as they come, but she does have the best intentions.

You see, her full-time job is to keep you safe. Comfortable. Out of harm's way. And it's an important job. Seriously.

If you'd just listen to her, you'd never take big risks. You would never have to face your fears or ruffle anyone's feathers. You would never screw something up or get burned by the bitterness of disappointment. You would never find yourself curled up in the fetal position on your bathroom floor crying an ugly cry after a massive, gnarly public failure. That's all she wants for you.

In fact, you'd never fail again.
(You wouldn't succeed either, but that's beside the point.)

That's it. That's Hilda's entire purpose for existing.

If you would just heed Hilda's messages, you would be able to stay snug and secure in your cozy little comfort zone from here until eternity. And while I know that sticking to your comfort zone is not good enough for you - demonstrated by the fact that you're reading this very book - you have to realize that this voice in your brain is just trying to do her job. Yes, her tactics and methods are atrocious - without question - but we've got to believe her heart is in the right place.

You're considering something risky and that freaks her out and she's scared. She's scared for you. Your feelings, your confidence, your ambition, your willpower, your integrity, your humility, and your heart. She wants to protect you from any and everything that poses a threat to one or more of those bits of you. The problem lies in the fact that most of what's most treasured and valuable in our lives sits squarely outside of the safe zone. But Hilda doesn't care. She's scared and she's ready to fight any threat that comes her way.

Now that you understand her motivations, perhaps some empathy is in order.

# How We're Gonna Shut Her Up

Okay, we can be empathetic now, but let's be real: Hilda needs to be stopped.

What would it feel like if . . .

- You tackled challenges and obstacles with confidence in yourself and your abilities?
- You forged your own path in life and said to hell with what others think?
- You charged through life with decisive and deliberate action toward your goals?
- You finished what you started, consistently, with tenacity and determination?
- You got out of your own damn way and unleashed your badassery onto the world?

All because you didn't participate in the Self-Sabotage Society anymore?!?

We're gonna name her. We're gonna write down her nonsense. We're gonna determine how your particular Hilda tends to sabotage you and then we're gonna undermine her motives + tactics. We're gonna inject a little logic to her craziness. Apply a little method to her madness, if you will. We're gonna smack her down with snappy comebacks that put her in her place.

Bottom line: we're gonna squash her self-sabotaging ways with some hardcore audacity.

# Name Your "Hilda"

In case you're wondering, no, you don't have to use the name *Hilda* to describe your inner naysayer. I am not the boss of you.

Other experts have dubbed the inner critic with interesting terms. Seth Godin gets all science-y and calls her your "reptilian lizard brain." Rick Carlson, author of "Taming Your Gremlin," likes to think of her as a fuzzy little monster that can't be fed after midnight. But calling her some sort of creature doesn't work for me. She's not a gremlin or a troll or a pissed off fairy - she's a bitchy little human that's getting in my way. Since Hilda is part of the human experience, she's basically human in my book. Get it?

Humanizing Hilda is important. Simply calling the voice in your head something highfalutin like the inner critic or inner saboteur only gives that Negative Nancy in your brain more credentials.

So let's give her (or him) a name.

About half of my clients over the years who resonated with the concept of Hilda have stuck with the name. The other half preferred to give her a new name that resonated more. She's been dubbed Gertrude, Agnes, Stella, Myrna, Eleanor, Olga, Psycho, Sydney, Buella, Shrillda, Mildred, Ethel, Maude, Phyllis, Herman, Henderson, Heinrich, Nick, Louise, Mister Picklebottom (one of my personal faves), and many, many more. Even Negative Nancy is up for grabs. Name your inner critic whatever the heck you want. The possibilities are endless.

## But pick a name.

For the men reading this book, which is probably about 14% of my readers based on super accurate data analysis conducted by me . . . guessing . . . almost arbitrarily, feel free to choose a man or a woman as your inner critic. In my coaching practice, about half of the men I've worked with have just stuck with Hilda. The choice is yours.

Got it? Good.

Now that you've named your Hilda, you just need some real, tangible tools to help you figure out why you self-sabotage, how you self-sabotage, why you actively self-sabotage when you're keenly aware that you are self-sabotaging, and what the hell you're going to do about it.

I'm going to give you some specific, tested techniques and mindset shifts to help you figure out why in the world you stand in the way of your own greatness, of your own audacity. I'm going to delve into stories of mine and of my clients to share with you exactly why this self-sabotage thing is truly the biggest obstacle we face in the pursuit of our wildest dreams.

By the time you finish this book, you'll be better able to identify where and why your Hilda shows up. More importantly, you'll be much more aware when she does and will more quickly and easily differentiate her defeatist nonsense from your truth. And you'll arm yourself with coaching techniques to combat Hilda's despicable tactics.

## So let's go!

# CHAPTER TWO

# Self-Sabotage 101

This is a self-help book, so I have to start this chapter with a definition. It's a rule. Don't question it.

*Self-sabotage* (verb) according to the mucky-mucks at Psychology Today is defined as:

> *"Behavior is said to be self-sabotaging when it creates problems and interferes with long-standing goals. These acts may seem helpful in the moment, but they ultimately undermine us, especially when we engage in them repeatedly."*

Self-sabotage is one of the most destructive forces in the human experience. We all do it. We all hate it. And far too many of us glorify it.

But what if we could choose to not be lazy? Just make a decision to do more? I don't mean more just for the sake of being busy, I mean more things that would align with who you want to be? Could we say no to stuff without feeling the side guilt? Can we show up exactly how we want without worrying how others may want us to be/act/talk/look/dress/etc? Can we step into the most extraordinary version of ourselves without apology and without regret?

It is high time that we cancel our subscription to the Self-Sabotage Society. Don't you agree?

## Hilda is a devious fear monger.

Marianne Williamson once famously said, "Our deepest fear is not that we are inadequate, our deepest fear is that we are powerful beyond measure." What a load of feel good BS.

That's right! I said it! It's BS.

Here's the thing: when you hear that, it gives you all of these feel good butterflies, and warm fuzzy feelings because it says that we are terrified of how great we can be. I get it. We're terrified of our own potential.

And while that sounds good on paper, it doesn't actually tell the truth. Because the truth is, we know that we are capable of greatness, right? We know we are capable of amazing, epic things.

What actually terrifies us, what scares the living daylights out of us, isn't that we have immense potential and immeasurable power. Our deepest fear is that we are incapable of stopping the self-sabotage so we can actually do something meaningful with all that potential and power.

Self-sabotage keeps us from achieving that potential! It keeps us from tapping into that power! It prevents us from becoming who we dream of being! And I, for one, think that's a helluva lot scarier than knowing we are super powerful. It's terrifying to realize that we have all this sexy, simmering potential; however, there is something in us, something wrong with us, that makes it so our self-sabotage is here forever. It's here to stay. And there is nothing we can do about it.

That's a horrifying thought in my mind. Haunting even.

The idea of Hilda, and all of the self-sabotaging nonsense inside is something that needs to be talked about. And it's something that needs to be talked about without the trite, "normal" Oprah Winfrey-approved quotes du jour. It's something that needs to be talked about head on, gloves off, eloquence be damned. It's time we answer some hard questions with straight answers.

Can we stop self-sabotaging? Is self-sabotage just a choice, or is there more to it? How many different ways do we self-sabotage? Are there trends? Why do we sabotage ourselves? Why do we get in our own way, and stay there? Is it possible to cut out self-sabotage? Is there a cure? And here's the biggie, if we stop self-sabotaging ourselves. What then? Then what are we capable of? What could be if we didn't sabotage ourselves ever again?

As I say that, I recognize a little bit of that Marianne Williamson fluff coming up, but let me be clear. I'm not afraid that I'm powerful beyond measure - I'm terrified that I'm standing in the way of that power and there's no way to stop. And if you're reading these pages, it's because you feel the same way. You feel like that voice inside of your head is ruling the world, and you want that to stop. Let's wake you up to all of the messages in your brain. Let's help you figure out how to split apart what Hilda is saying, and what you truly think. Let's teach you to think again. I know this sounds ridiculous, but we will. Because you need to think for yourself, not through Hilda. You must learn how to catch her when she's running amuck and running her mouth. Give her a donut or something to chew on!

So why the hell is self-sabotage so damn sexy? Well, we wouldn't do it if there wasn't something in it for us. It's convenient. It's comfortable. It's common. And it's highly addictive. And let's face it: it feels damn good.

I make my living helping people get out of their own freaking way. Yet the multitude of ways we self-sabotage never ceases to surprise and shock me.

We overthink.

We procrastinate.

We overburden ourselves with ideas and projects that we have little commitment to actually completing.

We set unrealistic, self-imposed timelines.

We hold ourselves to impossibly insane standards.

We procrastinate and then we make lists about the other things that we are procrastinating on and then we work on new project management tools in order to organize those lists of things we need to be doing and then that becomes a constant cycle of procrastination.

We are afraid of saying no.

We are afraid of saying no more.

We justify inaction with trite little phrases like "life got in the way."

We treat the unimportant noise in our life as constant emergencies that require our immediate attention, like a ringing phone or a text message or *gasp* an email notification.

We don't make time for family and friends or our own health and fitness goals.

We can't take compliments because they make us uncomfortable but we obsess over and over about the simplest piece of criticism.

Does any of this sound familiar?

If you're one of those people that is pretty darn good at beating yourself up for not meeting insanely high and next to impossible expectations, then digging into more capacity for greatness could turn into a massive heartache.

So let me ask you: what does this do for you? Seriously. What's in it for you to participate in all this self-flogging?

Is all this cruel self-treatment somehow inspiring and motivating you to work harder?

Is the quality of your work somehow gonna be better because you made it as difficult and emotionally challenging as humanly possible?

I'm 99.9% sure you didn't answer yes to any of those questions. Being routinely hard on yourself is doing absolutely nobody any good. In most cases, it's actually counterproductive. It's a colossal waste of time and energy that's keeping you from realizing your greatness. And it straight up feels sucky when you do it to yourself.

## So stop doing it!

90% of fixing this problem is simply raising your awareness, learning to catch yourself being hard on yourself, and noticing when you're upset that you're not doing enough. Taking a breath.

Or if you're up for some accountability, it's asking the people around you to listen for your defeatist habits and call you out on it.

Look. I'm not recommending you lower your expectations or slack off. That would be unaudacious and it's not what I'm all about. But you must give yourself credit for what you are doing and be kind to yourself as you chase your dreams. Otherwise, what's the freaking point?!

# Fueled by Fear

Your inner naysayer is fueled by fear. It's Hilda's favorite elixir. That's why she doesn't show up when you're doing the mundane, everyday things. She only awakens when you're about to (or are attempting to) do something that matters. When you're experiencing that perfect cocktail of exhilaration and slight terror about a new idea, Hilda perks up, flips through her reels of documentary footage, and splices together a screening designed to amplify the fear and tamper down the exhilaration.

Pick a fear. Any fear. She loves them all.

Fear of the unknown
Fear of judgment
Fear of rejection
Fear of missing out
Fear of embarrassment
Fear of change
Fear of rocking the boat
Fear of failure
Fear of success

And on and on and on.

The problem arises when these fears get in the way of you pursuing a scary (but totally badass) goal of yours, leaving you with nothing but a dusty old pipe dream.

Here's the good news: that fear is actually a good thing. When you feel it, it's your brain's way of saying, "Yo! This matters to you! Pay attention!" Fear keeps you on your toes, makes you aware of the circumstances, and shows you the obstacles that must be tackled. But we all know fear prefers to take a more leading role and tends to get in the way of pursuits of the more audacious manner. And that, my friend, has got to stop.

You must beat Hilda to the punch before she starts spewing her negativity your way.

In Elizabeth Gilbert's book, "Big Magic: Creative Living Beyond Fear," she wrote a letter of empathy to her fear before embarking on her newest creative adventure. Here's the beginning of that letter. As you read, mentally replace the word "fear" with "Hilda" and this is the empathetic approach to dealing with her.

> *"Dearest Fear: Creativity and I are about to go on a road trip together. I understand you'll be joining us, because you always do. I acknowledge that you believe you have an important job to do in my life, and that you take your job seriously. Apparently your job is to induce complete panic whenever I'm about to do anything interesting— and, may I say, you are superb at your job. So by all means, keep doing your job, if you feel you must. But I will also be doing my job on this road trip, which is to work hard and stay focused. And Creativity will be doing its job, which is to remain stimulating and inspiring. There's plenty of room in this vehicle for all of us . . . "*

You see? Compassion. Look, we don't want to kill Hilda. When we hear her, it means we are onto something spectacular. When she gets loud, it's basically a Bat Signal that we've stumbled onto something important. We need her around! We just have to shut her up faster, put her in the back seat, and refuse to allow her to run the show.

Remember, fear triggers Hilda. Every time you feel fear, your Hilda is just a few feet away, lurking in the shadows, awaiting her call to duty. Whether you're contemplating a juicy new goal, a risky leap into new territory, or a seismic shift in mindset, your comfort zone almost inevitably becomes threatened and fear bubbles up. Hilda is called to attention. She puts on her happy little "Risk Averse and Proud of It!" ball cap and gets to work, carefully crafting cruel and unusual ways to hold you hostage.

And you give in to her incessant noise eventually. You stay quiet and small and safe for a little while. Until your comfort zone gets boring and the vicious cycle starts all over again.

If you don't figure out how to break that cycle, bust through all that noise, and keep Hilda in check, you'll never truly know just what you're capable of.

# Hilda #IRL

Let's be real here. Hilda doesn't just make this shit up. All of these negative messages come from somewhere . . . and sometimes they come from the people who love you the most . . . in real life.

Hilda is an expert curator of defeatist thoughts and feelings. Since the day you were born, she's been carefully collecting, organizing, and filing away negative messages and bad advice shared by your family, friends, classmates, colleagues, partners, and even favorite television characters. These are your *Human Hildas*, and while they usually mean well, their messages can be especially damaging to your badassery. Hilda likes to remind you of their messages with an extra dose of guilt for not heeding their advice.

Who in your life is filling Hilda's library of nonsense? What defeatist thoughts and feelings has she claimed as her own?

Thanksgiving is often a time where you may be surrounded by your *Human Hildas*. Maybe your mom passes the mashed potatoes with a side of really loaded questions. Like "how's business?" "How's your love life?"

That's where it starts.

As you read through common Hildaisms in the coming chapters, some of the messages you read may sound eerily familiar or even take on the voice of some real live human beings in your life. That's totally normal. It doesn't mean you're a horrible person. And it doesn't mean that those people are bad people either. They want you to be safe - in the only ways they know how - but that can often leave you feeling small.

Although the feelings are the same, the tactics for dealing with Hilda versus your loved ones may need a tweak or two. I encourage you to tell Hilda to shut her pie hole; I do not necessarily recommend you say this to your sister. Unless she's like my sister . . . err, I digress.

Just something to keep in mind as you read further. I'll provide some modifications as we go.

# Onward.

# A Little Science to Back Me Up

Fellow nerds, this part is for you.

In addition to a decade of coaching experience, I'm also a total Positive Psychology nerd.

As I've demonstrated with Hilda, negative emotions have a tendency to pile up on each other. Fear begets fear begets even more fear. These negative feelings dump a bunch of negative chemicals (like cortisol and adrenaline) into your system which amplifies suckdom.

According to Dr. Barbara L. Frederickson, author of *Positivity: Groundbreaking Research Reveals How to Embrace the Hidden Strength of Positive Emotions, Overcome Negativity, and Thrive*, "Scientists say that emotions trigger specific action tendencies. Fear is linked with the urge to flee, anger with the urge to attack, disgust with the urge to expel, and so on." This almost guarantees failure.

These specific action tendencies yield two wins for Hilda:

1. you stay safe,
2. she gets in another *I told you so.*

Over time, it begets what Positive Psychologists call learned helplessness. How can this be reversed?

First, create a mindset conducive to change by accentuating the positive. Or as Dr. Frederickson puts it, "With positivity, you see new possibilities, bounce back from setbacks, connect with others, and become the best version of yourself." She calls this response "Broaden and Build."

Second, separate the present from Hilda's demented documentary. Dr. Martin E.P. Seligman, basically the Dumbledore of Positive Psychology, is an expert in both learned optimism and learned helplessness. In his research he, "found that people who believe that the causes of setbacks in their lives are temporary, changeable, and local do not become helpless." He goes on to point out that these people think, "it's going away quickly, I can do something about it, and it's just this one situation." Basically, they believe they have some semblance of control or influence over their current situation, even if their Hildas are mouthing off in the back of their minds.

Finally, take some freaking action. Dr. Sonja Lyubomirsky, author of *The How of Happiness: A New Approach to Getting the Life You Want*, points to "a study of people who resolved to carry through an important new goal for their New Year's resolution found that those who were confident that they could change were significantly more likely to maintain their resolutions over time. This is called a self-fulfilling prophecy, a belief that confirms itself, leading to its own fulfillment."

She goes on. "So, take action towards your goals, even when you have lingering doubts." Nothing squashes Hilda and her happy nonsense more than immediate action.

BOOM! The top experts back me up. (I love it when that happens.)

The bottom line: Self-sabotage is an inside job. It takes an insider to put an end to it. And that insider is YOU.

# Moving Forward

Even within the four BS Beliefs, Hilda is not a one-trick pony. She's carefully crafted and developed an arsenal of tactics designed to trigger or prolong your self-sabotage. I call these Hildaisms. These are the sassy phrases, questions, or one-two punches she has at her disposal that lead you to sabotage yourself once again.

## Who have you been hearing from lately?

In the pages that follow, I have categorized the most popular and common Hildaisms for each of these BS Beliefs: *I Can't, I Shouldn't, I Don't Know,* and *I Don't Wanna.* I've peppered in personal stories I just know you're going to resonate with the next time you hear your Hilda screaming in your head.

I invite you to dive into the Hildaisms that resonate with you the most and skip over the ones that don't, or if you prefer to read a book from cover-to-cover because that's how you roll, go ahead with your badass self. I'm not going to *should* all over you here. You do you.

## The premise of this book is rather ridiculous.

Yep. I freely admit it. It's kinda the point.

At first blush, the whole idea of naming the voice inside your brain like she's human feels like a silly little coaching exercise . . . dare I say "coachy." I'm a coach, and even I hate it when I become "too coachy." But I'm willing to get over this in order to tell you the truth.

Because learning how to differentiate Hilda's utter nonsense from your honest-to-goodness, know-it-in-your-gut truth takes practice. That's where this book comes in handy.

Without further ado, let's hear it, Hilda.

# Handy Dandy Hilda Cheat Sheet

## I Can't *Hilda*

Amplifies self-doubt and defeatism
Strikes at your sense of self from the inside
Makes you feel insecure
Convinces you to question your capability
Attacks your confidence

## I Shouldn't *Hilda*

Obsesses about the judgments of others
Strikes at your sense of self from the outside
Makes you feel self-conscious
Convinces you to change your behavior to please others
Attacks your possibilities

# Handy Dandy Hilda Cheat Sheet

## I Don't Know *Hilda*

Perpetuates inertia and indecision for as long as humanly possible
Avoids the starting line like the plague
Makes you feel stuck
Convinces you to second guess your every desire
Attacks your ambition

## I Don't Wanna *Hilda*

Justifies inaction and procrastination
Avoids the finish line like the plague
Makes you feel unfocused
Convinces you to avoid your goals
Attacks your tenacity

Want this cheat sheet in printable form? Visit: hildathebook.com

# CHAPTER THREE

# BS Belief #1: I Can't

First up, let's learn more about *I Can't* Hilda. She is on a mission to instigate copious amounts of self-doubt. This version of Hilda is a bully. She convinces even the most ambitious people around that they are unable to do the things that they want; that there's something wrong with them.

She brainwashes you into believing you are simply not as capable as everybody else. And even though this is not true, she constantly reinforces the idea that you are not good enough. This particular flavor of Hilda is focused on why you're not enough and constantly tries to sway you that you can't hack it. Unlike her evil stepsister, *I Shouldn't* Hilda, who is overly worried about perception and judgment from the outside world, *I Can't* Hilda prefers to rip you up from the inside. Even if everybody on the outside supports and loves you and thinks you're completely capable - awesome even - this Hilda has you thinking otherwise. By the way, she's collected plenty of evidence.

*I Can't* Hilda wants to make sure you feel inadequate in every sense of the word, that you feel incapable of doing something that matters. That you straight up don't have it in you. That you don't have the skills, don't have the ability, don't have the aptitude, don't have the temperament to make things happen...to do what it is you want to do to change the world.

Self-doubt is a natural part of the human experience. But where the heck does it come from?

As we start out into the world, we're pretty darn confident. As toddlers, we figure out how to crawl and slowly stand up and then eventually walk because we're absolutely determined to pull it off. Our tenacity and drive to get places faster and grab things quicker keep us going, even when we fall down. I don't think I've ever met a toddler who thought, "Hmm, I can't do that. It hurts. I can't ever walk." Usually what they're thinking is "I just haven't figured it out yet."

As kids get a little older, around elementary school age, most of them hang on to this "I can" attitude. I have nieces and nephews that age and I watch them with awe. If you ask them, "Hey, will you dance for me?" or, "will you draw me a picture?" they do it immediately. Why? Because they absolutely believe that they can. They believe that they're dancers, that they're artists, that they can do those things because well, frankly, they can. The kicker is they are not consumed with how well they do those things. In fact, my nieces and nephews are proud of every artistic expression that they create. Good, bad, ugly, or even entirely indecipherable.

As they become tweens and teens, something changes. Now, I'm sure a scientist or psychologist would tell you specifically what happens when and that this is part of the journey of becoming an adolescent, but this seems to be where Hilda starts paying attention. It's annoying to me, kind of pisses me off, that Hilda was not documenting all of those times when we were tenacious and driven and filled with creative confidence. She seems to have been waiting to hit the "record" button until now. And suddenly, there's something about you that's missing, inferior, lacking, or all together uncool.

On top of that, there's this strange part of adolescence where we're all engaged in this bizarre tug of war, trying to figure out how we can stand out and fit in simultaneously. This is an impossible, yet universal feat. Finally, tack on obsessively worrying about appearances and we are left with the conclusion that we can't measure up.

And I get it. Part of growing up is experiencing self-doubt and figuring out how to deal with it, but for some of us Hilda makes our entire documentary all about it - about not measuring up, about not being capable, about something being wrong with us, about the things we cannot do. Unfortunately, this noise tends to follow us right into adulthood.

Here's an important reminder: just because you hear *I Can't* Hilda in your brain, it doesn't mean you have incredibly low self-esteem or that there's something really wrong with you. It means you're human and it means you want something. As I said in the introduction, Hilda only shows up and rears her ugly head when you're about to do something that matters. Remember her goals: to slow you down, to keep you small, and to remind you that this is too risky.

But you *can* stop sabotaging yourself. You can stop getting in your own way. You can make spectacular things happen. If you have the right tools.

# Who Do You Think You Are?

Christopher is a fabulous, patient, and passionate Pilates instructor that specializes in working with what he lovingly calls his broken people - people with chronic pain, injuries, loss of mobility, or other physical impairments. Most of them have never done Pilates before, but they learn to love it. His approach to this work is life changing for this niche of people.

Christopher is working on a book designed to introduce Pilates to a global audience. And despite how phenomenal he is at his work and how much his clients sing his praises, the moment he decided to start writing this book, Herman (his Hilda) started in on him . . .

> *You aren't qualified enough.*
> *What are all of your colleagues gonna think?*
> *You don't know what you're doing.*
> *This book is unnecessary.*
> *Who do you think you are?*

Just about every badass I've ever talked to has had bouts with Impostor Syndrome. It's a particularly evil way that Hilda infects us. Impostor Syndrome is probably the most well-known Hilda tactic in the land. American psychologists Dr. Pauline Clance and Dr. Suzanne Imes coined this phrase back in 1978. They observed that despite ample evidence that highly-motivated high achievers had earned their stripes and qualifications, many of them still "live in fear of being 'found out' or exposed as frauds." It's when you have that nagging feeling and nasty thinking that everyone is going to think you're a big, fat poser who has no business calling herself an "expert" in anything. Hilda skillfully makes you think this by asking the most popular Hildaism of all time . . .

# Who do you think you are?

If you've never experienced this, stop reading. Move onto some dancing kittens on YouTube or something. I don't want to trigger your self-conscious to start thinking these nasty thoughts. (And by the way, you are my hero. May I get your autograph?)

If you do resonate with what I'm talking about, well, welcome to the club. This is one of the main reasons people seek to get certified in things – it provides some sort of gold star of social proof that you're qualified to do the thing you purport yourself to do. And it works. For a while at least. Right up until the point when you decide to stretch yourself beyond your comfort zone again. Amiright?!

> *Thought: Hilda makes you question your talent and abilities.*
>
> *Feeling: You get all kinds of worried of being exposed as an impostor.*
>
> *Action: You shrink yourself like any real impostor would.*

Obviously countless books have been written to combat impostor syndrome at a deep level. You'll find my faves in the Appendix of this book. But for our purposes, you need a badass counteraction to shut down this thinking and get back on track. Simplified, the key to winning the battle over impostor syndrome and *I Can't* Hilda is to collect evidence to the contrary.

## Your Turn

Put another way, the best comeback to the snide, rhetorical Hildaism *Who do you think you are?* is to simply answer her freaking question. Tell her in no uncertain terms exactly the kind of badass that you think (ahem, you *know*) you are.

# You're Not Qualified

Joy, my first client from the Philippines, is the MommyProofing Coach. A mother of two, she's on a mission to eradicate "Mommy Guilt." She's spent loads of time building up her identity and brand while maintaining her roles as wife and mother. She's faced and fought the entrepreneurial struggles of time management, money woes, and work-life balance, which created the perfect opportunity for Hilda to sneak in.

She is currently working on fully owning her expertise. She only recently named herself the MommyProofing Coach, and has been developing some recognition around that concept.

Yet as much as she's kicking butt and taking names, Hilda is right there filling her head with a bunch of doubt. She once shared with me in her coaching session that Hilda has a very particular way of getting to her with a particular line of questioning . . .

> *Are you sure you're an expert on this?*
> *Just because you have a kid, it doesn't mean you speak for mommies everywhere.*
> *You're way out of your element.*
> *Who gave you permission to call yourself such a thing?*

Joy and I unpacked what Hilda is really doing when she questions our expertise. *I Can't* Hilda dreads when you put yourself out there. Understandably, it's freaking terrifying to go out and declare to the world, "I am The MommyProofing Coach" or "I am The Audacity Coach" or {insert whatever it is you are purporting yourself to be}. But there is a tactical workaround.

*Thought: Hilda gets you to question your expertise.*

*Feeling: You become terrified of putting yourself out there.*

*Action: You don't put yourself out there. Hilda enjoys celebratory bonbons.*

You must become relentlessly obsessed with your thought leadership; your area of expertise. Explore every facet of your field. Become both a student and teacher. Perpetually learning, questioning, and gaining experience is the ultimate way to silence Hilda. She can't argue your expertise when you're the most learned, living library in the room - and have research to back it up.

## Your Turn

How will you develop and own your qualifications? What does it look like to become relentlessly obsessed with your work on this planet?

# You Suck

You've failed. If you're human and even the least bit ambitious, you've experienced at least some form of failure. It's part of the human experience.

No reason to deny it.

*I Can't* Hilda loves that you've failed. It gives her stupid documentary low moments to capture and even more footage for her arsenal. She takes every failure you've ever experienced, big or small, and catalogs it for future use against you. When you're starting to think you might be ready for something new and exciting, she busts out another screening of these failure experiences until you remember what it feels like to fail. Our demented documentarian is on a mission to convince us that we're just a bunch of walking failures waiting to happen.

Remember: she doesn't highlight the moments when we reigned victorious. All past failures are amplified and internalized. All past successes are quickly shortchanged and minimized.

> *Thought: Hilda reminds you of a failure from your past.*
>
> *Feeling: You experience the bitter feelings of defeat all over again.*
>
> *Action: You avoid putting yourself at risk of another failure. Hilda wins again!*

## So yes. You've failed before. So what?

Maybe you've risked it all and lost already.

Maybe you've belly flopped into failure more than once, and it's made you extra cautious.

"I'm not going there again!" squeals your bruised little ego.

Ask yourself which is scarier: jumping into the unknown, or jumping back into something you've failed at previously? Why?

Enough hemming and hawing. Stop overanalyzing your choices to death. In order to take the risk and leap, it's imperative to honor your past successes, too.

---

## Your Turn

What are three successes that Hilda wants you to forget? What did you think, feel, and do during and immediately following those experiences? How can you mirror that now?

*"I have an everyday religion that works for me.
Love yourself first, and everything else falls into line.
You really have to love yourself to get anything done
in this world."*

*~ Lucille Ball*

# You're Not Worthy

I ask a lot of questions in the Audacity LAB. Every single day, I post different prompts and quizzes and challenges for my community of badasses. I work really hard on these questions recognizing most people do not answer them in that public forum. But these questions do linger in the backs of their minds. Some of these questions can yield immeasurable breakthroughs.

Last summer, I posed a challenge that really shook up one of my one-on-one Audacity Coaching clients . . .

"Give yourself a compliment. A genuine one. One that makes your heart sing a little."

"What's the best thing about being YOU?"

Many people didn't think twice and answered these questions quickly and publicly. But when *I Can't* Hilda is running the show, the gloves come off. Simply reading these questions twisted my client up and brought her to tears. She immediately thought, "there's nothing that's the best thing about being me. There's nothing worthy of a compliment. I've got nothing."

Now as much as these questions really shook her confidence, this chick is audacious and wasn't going to let them go unanswered. She reached out and let me know that on her next coaching agenda she wanted to discuss how this landed for her.

I knew there were really great answers to my questions waiting just under the surface, hiding behind her Hilda. I also knew I was going to have to push into some ridiculously uncomfortable territory in order to get down and dirty into the noise Hilda was spewing here.

I asked her first, "How did it feel when you read the challenge?" She immediately started telling me what she was thinking and how she reacted, assuming that's the response I was expecting.

I reiterated the question. "When you read these questions, how did you *feel*?" This time she really heard me.

After a deep breath, she burst into tears. She admitted to herself she immediately felt small and insignificant. So I asked her more. I asked her how she wanted to feel.

After a dramatic and somewhat comical exasperated sigh, she smiled and shook her head knowing that I was taking her yet again into the deep ocean of uncomfortableness. She couldn't answer.

Read that sentence again. She had no idea how she wanted to feel.

> *Thought: Hilda convinces you there's nothing about you that's compliment-worthy.*
>
> *Feeling: Your confidence plummets and you feel an epic wave of self-doubt and despair.*
>
> *Action: You spend the rest of the afternoon beating yourself up for being less than compliment-worthy.*

When we are so shoulder deep in the BS Beliefs that we can't do something, we can't see the forest for the trees. We're so consumed in self-doubt that we lose touch with our emotions. I recognize this is a paradox because when you're feeling self-doubt you feel like you're nothing but a clusterscrew of raw emotions. And yet in this moment, my client had no idea what she wanted to feel.

You must know what you want to feel in order to defeat this particular trick up Hilda's sleeve.

Do you want to feel happy, empowered, inspired, motivated, elated, excited, challenged, engaged, fascinated, intrigued, confident, loved, alive, grateful, joy, interested, serenity, hope, surprised, delighted, admired, creative, decisive, calm, clear, appreciated, positive, powerful, noble, optimistic, focused, free, frisky, luxurious, worthy, zestful, strong, unlimited, proud, warm, invigorated, hopeful, energized, enlightened, peaceful, passionate, content, eager, refreshed? Something else?

If you don't know how you want to feel, you are giving away your power.

Once I offered up a few examples to kickstart her thinking, she was able to dig in and start stating some emotions. Pride proved to be the most important choice for her. With this in mind, we returned to the challenge that started it all. Now she had her answer:

*The best thing about being me is that I'm honest without being hurtful.*

Her snickering smile turned into a genuine one. Her body language softened. Immediately she felt great. Honesty is one of her top values, and the fact that she's consistently honest but not hurtful gave her a sense of pride.

## Your Turn

What do you want to feel? What can you do right now to create that suite of feelings?

# You're Just Not Good Enough

Have you ever had a performance review? You know, where your boss pulls you aside once a year. They tell you how you did and write up all of your accomplishments and your areas of improvement. It is not a fun task for the boss nor the employee, no matter how great you are. As a high achiever, I guess your reviews have been pretty stellar. However, this is an optimal opportunity for *I Can't* Hilda to swoop in and have her way with you. As you read through your performance review, your eyes zoom in on the negative, of course. It could be a glowing review. It could offer a huge promotion, maybe even a raise! But no, your brain fixates on "The one thing you could improve on this year is . . ." And boom!

That is it.

That is all you hear.

That is all you read.

## You are not enough.

There's your focus.

Well, that's Hilda's focus actually. She is clearly leading the show. This is not just for people with day jobs, either. Same goes for those in the entrepreneurial space. I know people who have published books that have been extraordinarily successful and they obsess about their solitary 1-star review, despite hundreds of positive 4- and 5-star reviews. I know restaurateurs who only respond to people who leave less-than-stellar feedback on their Yelp page.

> *Thought: Hilda points out and magnifies your areas for improvement as massive failures.*
>
> *Feeling: You feel humiliated and lose most (if not all) of the positive feelings you had about the other 98% of the review.*
>
> *Action: You obsess about how to fix the problem areas instead of exploring ways to amplify your strengths.*

Whenever this particular Hildaism pops in your brain, remind yourself that Hilda is not the boss of you. And once you take back over as the boss of you, accentuate the positive. We must shift this mindset. We must put down the measuring stick and realize we are never going to measure up to Hilda's expectations of perfection. We very well may suck at first but that self-imposed nagging voice in our head has no right to give us a performance review anyhow. And then we must activate. If you're lacking important know-how, take a class. Ask people who have the know-how what steps they took to learn it. Fall down the rabbit hole of watching YouTube videos. Do something, anything really, to move yourself forward.

Remember, you *are* enough. You are more than enough. And if you're like most of the people I know, you're probably at least a little too much. The proof is in all the positives. Look there.

## Your Turn

How does your "enoughness" stuff show up? What negative review or other hiccup has drawn far too much of your (and Hilda's) attention? List out all the positives that prove the contrary and focus on those.

# They're Just Being Polite

Clearly, filmmaker J.J. Abrams is at the top of his game. He's one of the most recognized names in Hollywood, and it's well deserved. I mean, this is the genius behind LOST and the man the Star Trek fandom has adopted as its leader. On top of all that, Disney and George Lucas recently decided to entrust one of the most beloved movie franchises in history to him: Star Wars.

In a recent interview, J.J. talked about the experience of screening a rough cut of the film for the top four Disney executives. Can you imagine it? He's sitting in the dark, in silence, watching the people who pay the bills watch his movie. And this is a rough cut - no CGI or sound effects yet. He must have been crawling out of his own skin in excitement and terror.

At the end of the screening, he braced himself for the worst but the executives were thrilled! (Duh.) They showered him with all kinds of wonderful praise. But, instead of being over-joyed, his Hilda came out to play. And I imagine she said something like this "They spent $4 billion on THAT? They didn't really like it. In fact, they probably hated it. They are just being polite."

*Thought: Hilda instills disbelief that this positive feedback could actually be true.*

*Feeling: You become self-conscious and uncomfortable.*

*Action: You refuse to trust anyone who pays you a compliment. In fact, you assume they are lying through their teeth.*

Again, this is a man at the top of his career, the very top of his game, and even he has moments of intense self-doubt. The truth is, it doesn't matter how successful you become or how much praise you receive - like the Empire, *I Can't* Hilda strikes back. And this is where J.J. once again proves exceptional - he heard his Hilda but didn't give up. He got back to work. He made his already great movie even better.

Is this a challenge for you? Do you suck at hearing and accepting compliments?

## Your Turn

Who is your most consistent source of praise? What does Hilda do with their compliments? What do you need to put in place so you can more easily accept praise?

# There's No Way You'll Pull This Off

Let's say you've decided to go all in with your professional speaking career, and you have secured a TED Talk. A freaking TED Talk. It's real. It's on. This shit is actually happening. You tell the world, brag to your friends, do everything you can to build buzz around this epic accomplishment in the making, and right on cue, here's Hilda.

*There's no way you can pull this off.*
*I can't do this.*
*I'm so not ready for the big time.*
*I just know I'm gonna fall flat on my face and humiliate myself.*
*And it will be on film.*
*My sister will see it.*
*My church will see it.*
*I will be shunned from my church.*
*My grandmother won't love me anymore.*

Setting goals is the easy part. Trusting that you've got the capability to pull it off? Yeah, that's a whole other thing. Hilda sabotages you this time by hitting the brakes hard. Suddenly, you find yourself planning to fail.

## Stop that. Immediately.

In one of my favorite ooey-gooey movies, *Stepmom*, there is a part where Julia Roberts does a little life coaching with her new stepdaughter. She says very clearly, "As I see it, there are two choices: on the one hand you can sit here, crying, in the cold, by yourself, and the other you can do something about it . . . crying, do something about it, crying, do something about it . . . so what do you choose?" I love that stubborn pursuit of action. Just deciding, *yes, I'm gonna do something about it.*

Rent "Stepmom." Bring tissues.

Instead of planning for all the ways you could fail, let's look at the other side of the coin: What would wild success look like?

> *Thought: Hilda tricks you into expecting colossal failure.*
>
> *Feeling: You freak out, feel unsure, and brace yourself for that impending failure.*
>
> *Action: You shut down and prepare to fail.*

Now reality typically resides somewhere in between wild success and epic failure. In this example, reality might be nailing all your most important talking points, getting a solid and professional video afterwards, and booking future speaking gigs based on this one epic, fantastic 18-minute talk. Once you know what realistic success looks like, you can plan and prepare accordingly.

Ninety percent of the battle is recognizing when you are planning to fail, checking yourself, and figuring out how to plan for success instead.

## Your Turn

What would success look like? What do you need to put in place to make that success more easily attainable?

# You're Just Not Relationship Material

While Hilda tends to work overtime to sabotage your professional goals, your love life is certainly not off limits. For some people, Hilda is loudest and most pervasive in this particular life compartment.

If you're single, Hilda likes to get into your head about your dating life.

> *You're incomplete without a partner.*
> *You always pick the wrong people.*
> *You're too old or ugly or fat or blonde or _____ to meet someone.*
> *My family members will hate him.*
> *Your standards and expectations are just too high.*
> *You're not lovable.*
> *Face it: you're just not relationship material.*

When you're consumed with this kind of noise, you're worried about there being some truth to the facts. That there is something wrong with you or something about you that makes you unlovable.

For those of you who have already coupled up, you're not exempt from this happy nonsense. Hilda's noise can still be part of your romantic life, too.

> *I wonder what he's thinking.*
> *He is falling out of love with you.*
> *You need to be having more sex if your relationship is going to make it.*
> *You complain too much. You should be more agreeable.*
> *You should be jealous of all the attention he gives whatshername.*
> *He's going to cheat on you if you're not a better wife.*
> *You've gained a few pounds and he won't love you if you get too fat.*
> *You should be worried about your marriage.*

I blame the movies and television shows like *Sex and The City*. Let's face it, chick flicks are just another form of #IRL Hilda. The fantasy of a cinematic romance may feel really yummy, but works against us and feeds your Hilda. And don't get me started on self-help books around relationships and love! There's something about relationship self-help books that makes us feel bad. So many of these representations of relationships convince you that you are the reason you're still single or you are the reason that your relationship isn't cinematically perfect. And these *Sex and The City* mindsets have snuck into our brains turning complaining about our relationships into our favorite form of entertainment.

> *Thought: Hilda convinces you there's something uniquely wrong with you.*
>
> *Feeling: You feel unlovable and super sad that you've not experienced a Hollywood romance.*
>
> *Action: You sabotage your relationships because they rarely measure up to the Hollywood fantasy.*

Hilda plays with all of these ideas beautifully. The *Sex and The City* mindset has convinced you that you need to look like Carrie Bradshaw, act like a hotshot New York lawyer, think like a debutante who is desperate to marry, have all the trappings of a rich, fancy-class public relations mogul. Only then can you experience love and companionship and intimacy.

I call BS on that.

Love and cinematic perfection are not happy bedfellows.

Look, I'm not a relationship expert so I certainly don't have all the answers. But I know Hilda has no business sticking her nose in your love life. You partner/future partners will appreciate it if you find a way to leave her out of your relationships. This means it's more important than ever to differentiate her *I Can't* naysaying noise (and *I Shouldn't* and *I Don't Know* and *I Don't Wanna* messages for that matter) from your truth. Yours. Not Carrie's. Not Charlotte's. Not Miranda's. And definitely not Samantha's.

## Your heart. Your needs. Your truth.

Note: For some of you, *I Shouldn't* may be the more successful saboteur in the relationship realm. Perhaps your family and friends are very vocal and strong in their opinions about your love life and your human Hildas feed your inner Hilda. Maybe you worry about choosing the right dates or partners based on some arbitrary societal expectations. While the Hildaisms come from a different root, the solution remains the same.

---

## Your Turn

How does Hilda screw with your romantic life? What comeback can you say to her the next time she points her negativity toward your love life?

# Why Bother?

So you go to a networking event in the hopes of making some new friends. Maybe you've just moved to a new city or changed careers. As much as you enjoy meeting people online via social media, you crave interactions with actual three-dimensional human beings in the same space. And even though you want to meet new people, it takes an incredible amount of courage and gumption for you to make the trip in the first place.

Not knowing a single soul, you arrive with a smile and start making your way around the room. After a deep breath, you sidle up to a couple of people who were chatting and cautiously insert yourself into the conversation. After exchanging intros, elevator pitches, and some agonizing small talk, each superficial conversation ends with you standing alone.

After several rounds of this nonsense, you decide to tuck your tail between your legs and sneak out of the event early. Hilda leaps into action.

> *I told you not to attend these things.*
> *You suck at networking, remember?*
> *Nobody thinks you're funny or charming.*
> *Stick with your online peeps who can mute you when you're talking.*
> *You're just not friend-worthy.*
> *Why even bother?*

Now, of course, making connections online isn't something that you were able to do instantly. It happened over time, after several interactions, slowly, but surely. But for some reason, Hilda has convinced you that you are not worth knowing. That you are not likable. That you are not lovable. That you are still that kid no one wants to play hopscotch with.

Uh, nothing could be further from the truth.

I have no idea why it's so much harder to make friends as adults, but it is. When we were little, we could knock on the door of a new neighbor and say, "I noticed there's a kid about my age who lives here. Can she come out and play?" That doesn't work quite as well in adulthood.

Okay. So what?

When you leave the event early, only talk to the people you already know, or otherwise throw up your hands in a 'why bother' defeat, Hilda wins.

> *Thought: Hilda busts out documentary footage of the last networking event where you crashed and burned.*
>
> *Feeling: You experience the awkwardness that accompanied the last networking event you attended all over again.*
>
> *Action: You go through the motions of fake smiles, forceful handshakes, and canned elevator pitches without trying to make meaningful connections. Or if she really freaked you out, you bail on the event all together.*

This is an opportunity to dig deep into why you are attempting this in the first place. Just like when Hilda asked you, "Who do you think you are?," it's time for some comebacks. This is your chance to answer her stupid question: Why bother?

*Because this is important to me.*
*This will give me a leg up on my job search.*
*This will allow me to have a social life beyond work.*

*I'm a lovely person that's worth getting to know.*
*I want to get involved in my community.*

With comebacks like these, there is no way Hilda will be able to convince you that you can't.

---

## Your Turn

Sooooo . . . why bother? Answer the question in no uncertain terms. Why is this worth the effort?

# You Cannot Be Serious

I recently attended a conference of professional speakers called Rock the Stage. It was put together by one of my personal professional speaking heroes, Josh Shipp. It was one of those epic life-changing experiences.

I've got to be honest with you, when I attended there was one topic on the agenda that I was not planning to really listen to - How to Get on Television. Then Darren Kavinoky took the stage.

His opening video was flashy and showcased all of the different television programs he'd been featured on. It also had a trailer for his upcoming television program that he is producing himself. Then he shared his personal story and I found myself hanging on his every word. He was mesmerizing.

He said that getting on television would allow me to "amplify my voice and accelerate my message." I was intrigued. He explained how getting on television with a book like mine was easier than I think. I was fascinated. Then he asked us to list what three national television shows we would like to appear on with our message. I was flabbergasted. An emotional skirmish between my excitement and Hilda ensued.

I thought, "Can you imagine how many more people I could reach if I had the opportunity to introduce Hilda to the world on The Today Show?"

*You can't be serious.*

"Don't you think that Good Morning America would find my slightly irreverent take on the inner critic perfect for their viewers?"

*You're kidding me, right?*

"Can you see me explaining why Hilda means well to Ellen? Think she'll dance with me?"

*What a pipe dream.*

You hear a speaker like Darren and Hilda lets her guard down for the briefest of moments. You start thinking bigger, much bigger. You want to do more. You want to have more. You want to be more. You allow yourself to dream for a moment, even a split second, to explore new levels of possibility. But as soon as Hilda gets back from her coffee break, she shits all over your enthusiasm with fancy versions of the phrase, *You can't be serious.*

Hell yes I'm serious!

Don't let her take away the seriousness of your dreams. Be serious about it and make it happen.

> *Thought: Hilda convinces you this opportunity is way out of your league.*
>
> *Feeling: You feel inadequate and small.*
>
> *Action: You decide it's not worth the rejection. If you don't put yourself out there, they can't reject you, right?*

Take me for example. I would reach out to Darren and ask for his help on pitching The Today Show, Good Morning America, and Ellen. I would polish my pitch, get it professionally edited, and follow through with all sorts of relentless optimism. I would not stop there. I would also pitch to other shows from local cable access to the syndicated news. I would be serious simply by choosing to take this goal seriously, and choosing to think bigger.

Furthermore, whenever you hear the particular Hildaism of, "You can't be serious," you can shut her up by pointing out that other people are living your dream right now and ask the question, "Why not me?"

A pipe dream is only that if there's no real action behind it.

I'll wave at you from The Today Show.

## Your Turn

Next time you want to do something and hear this Hildaism, ask yourself the three whys . . .

Why?
Why not?
Why not me?

*"Whether you think you can, or you think you can't – you're right."*

*~ Henry Ford*

# You CAN

Henry Ford's infamous quote leaves little room for interpretation.

It's so true. The very hard truth is that you are the only person who can determine whether or not you can do something. Other people can believe in you, cheer you on, coach you through your negative self-talk, and push you to keep going, but they cannot do all the believing for you.

It's an inside job.

Remember, *I Can't* Hilda is a bully and a professional doubt inserter. So sneaky. Hildaisms are deviously designed to leave little drops of self-doubt all around your brain. As these self-doubt droplets accumulate, Hilda slowly but surely drowns your confidence.

## *I Can't* is total BS.

To change your belief about your abilities, you need to change your thought from "can't" to "can" and then assume you will. I'm not gonna sugarcoat it for you: this can be a really, really hard habit to break and it will probably not happen overnight. However, it may be one of the most important tips yet.

When you accept the BS Belief that you can't do something, you choose failure. You are actively sabotaging your greatness. And this can't happen - because the world needs your greatness.

So stop listening to Hilda and all of her obnoxious *I Can't* noise. You're so much better than that. Either you believe you can or you believe you can't. And which way you choose to believe is completely up to you.

Choose better.

# CHAPTER FOUR

# BS Belief #2: I Shouldn't

A llow me to introduce our next professional saboteur. This Hilda isn't so consumed with what she can and can't do, she is really worried about what she should or should not do. She's obsessed with what your parents will think, and what your neighbors will think, and what your friends will think, and what your spouse will think, and what your boyfriend or girlfriend, or anybody outside of you will think about what you are doing. In fact, she often gets consumed with what *they* will think - even when you don't know who the hell *they* actually represent.

*I Shouldn't* Hilda is paranoid. She constantly worries about how what you want and what you do will be perceived. Is it sexy enough? Is it good enough? Does it compare to such-and-such or so-and-so? This is the Kardashian way of life, trying to keep up with somebody else, or keep up with appearances at least.

*I Shouldn't* Hilda has a toxic obsession with being judged - but is pretty darned judgmental herself. She trains your brain to react emotionally to specific trigger words, phrases, or experiences to knock you on your ass. Sometimes even the most common words set off huge, mortifying reactions.

If this is your predominant Hilda, it can be embarrassing to even admit it. Most people that I've worked with who have *I Shouldn't* Hildaisms plaguing them day-to-day feel they are the only ones walking the earth with this happy nonsense in their brain. It often looks like this:

Maybe you're in dire need of a day off. More than anything you could use a morning to read in bed, lunch out with your friends, a mani/pedi appointment, and a trip to the beach. Or maybe you're jazzed about a new business venture, a bold new idea, or a budding relationship. Or maybe, whatever it is, you're ready to take that big juicy risk that lights your soul on fire.

Then, you're barraged with an onslaught of *I Shouldn'ts*:

> *People are gonna laugh at you.*
> *You're gonna screw it up.*
> *I mean, you'll never live up to expectations.*
> *Aren't you happy enough?*
> *Shouldn't you just be grateful for what you have?*
> *Why are you so selfish?*
> *Your new idea is going to flop and you'll embarrass the heck out of yourself.*

*I Shouldn't* Hilda brings up memories of high school. She is like the head cheerleader or that nagging parent figure or that obnoxious teacher/librarian with a bun - don't know why she wore a bun, but she always did. If your go-to Hilda is the *I Shouldn't* Hilda, then your mindset may not have graduated when you did.

You want to make sure you never upset anyone and everybody approves of and validates what you're doing. And because that's pretty much impossible, Hilda is going to win because she repeatedly convinces you the opinions of others matter more than your own.

It isn't just about blind followership. That's how she shows up for many people. Scary, right?

If *I Shouldn't* Hilda is doing her job, you will only do things that you know without a doubt you can do really, really well. You won't even attempt something that might embarrass you. In this section of the book, we'll dive deeper into fears like "People might laugh at you," "Your goals aren't good enough," "Your goals are too selfish," "Why can't you just be grateful for what you already have," "Why can't you just be more like so-and-so," and "Why can you never compete with whatsherface?" We will confront the big, horrible idea that we might embarrass ourselves, because to Hilda, embarrassment equals death. We'll battle the Hilda that says "If you don't apply to the job, they can't reject you" and "If you don't audition for the show, they can't say no." "Don't speak your mind." "Don't have an opinion." "Don't even think about dancing."

Obeying this Hilda is no way to live. You can and *should* move past it.

"And the day came when the risk to remain tight in a bud was more painful than the risk it took to blossom."

~ Anais Nin

# Oh, Behave

It was an introductory session with a brand new client. As we were getting to know each other, she shared with me a sentence that took my breath away. She said, "I suffer from Perfect Child Syndrome."

It took me a moment to process this.

I had heard of Impostor Syndrome (we discussed it earlier in this very book!). However, Perfect Child Syndrome was a phrase I never heard before, but understood instantly. I used to call it the "Good Girl Syndrome," or the "Good Girl Problem," but this is so much juicier, so much more spot on.

Many of us grew up as the peacemakers of our families. We were the ones who had to keep everyone on point and making sense. We were (and often still are) the ones to make sure there was no conflict in the house at any time. Any discord made us squeamish and uncomfortable. We just wanted to be the perfect kid. The kind of kid people would say, "oh, you're such a good girl or boy" about. The kind of kid who deserves praise, exudes pride, and never makes a freaking mistake. Eventually, this desire becomes a syndrome. The need to be a model sister, a perfect son, or employee of the month, permeates every fiber of us. So everything falls under one umbrella - be good. Behave.

This is tremendously painful and an impossible standard to live up to, because being good means you will never get to disagree again, right? You'll never quarrel, you'll never question anything, you'll never argue a point, never express an opinion - you'll never show an emotion. Because you'll never cause conflict and guess what - you'll never shine either!

*Thought: Hilda reminds you that you are supposed to be perfect and not supposed to make mistakes . . . ever.*

*Feeling: You fall down a deep dark hole of humiliation and become even more afraid to make mistakes.*

*Action: You play by the rules, do as you're told, and stay in your lane. Hilda has got you where she wants you.*

There's a treacherous shame spiral Hilda guides you on if you suffer from Perfect Child Syndrome. First, you make a mistake. "Oh dear God, you made a mistake! The world is about to end, so prepare yourself!" Once you've flubbed up, BOOM! Hilda stores away her new evidence proving you screw up from time to time; you are flawed and/or failure-prone and therefore a total screwup. No more perfect child. You may as well become a hermit.

See how quickly that goes from minor misstep to major meltdown in 60 seconds or less?

Here's the newsflash for my Perfect Children out there:

1. You're human. Hate to break it to you.
2. This expectation of perfection is sabotaging your success.
3. It's perfectly normal that you're imperfectly human. It's worthy of celebration even.
4. You need to embrace the middle ground between impossible perfection and hot freaking mess. You live your life somewhere in the middle, because of (see #1).

## Mistakes won't kill you. Promise.

## Your Turn

Are you ready to hang up your Perfect Child cape once and for all? How can you let go of your need to behave as expected and simply be the wonderfully imperfect and extraordinary person in progress you are?

*"Those who mind don't matter, and those who matter don't mind!"*

*~ Dr. Seuss*

# They're All Gonna Laugh at You

Ever been in this situation? You are in a group of people - meeting at work, out with friends, whatevs - and someone asks a question. You immediately muster a thought or an opinion, but as it's bubbling up to the surface, you hold yourself back.

Maybe you're thinking . . .

> *You know what, that's so unoriginal and everyone is already thinking the same thing.*
> *Don't be Captain Obvious here.*
> *This idea is half-baked at best.*
> *What if everyone thinks that I'm dumb?*

Or perhaps you're thinking, "Man, I have a really strong opinion about this and I'm betting lots of people here disagree with me, so I better keep my trap shut for the good of everyone."

Hilda constantly criticizes to keep you from contributing. She tries to shut you up because she needs to keep you comfortable, living by default, coloring within the lines, not rocking the boat. Pick an idiom, any idiom. She busts out the red pen to edit and mute you so you stay silent.

Remember, she means well. Even though she's annoying and irksome and frustrating and holding you back, her motivations are very genuine. She's a thoughtful one. She wants to make sure you don't screw up and embarrass yourself (and her).

But here's some breaking news - in order to live audaciously, you have to screw up. You have to break down a few doors and maybe get into a few disagreements. And you absolutely, positively must not allow her to keep shushing you. It's not doing anybody any favors. It's more likely causing problems.

> *Thought: Hilda shoots down your initial thoughts, opinions, and ideas as half-baked.*
>
> *Feeling: You get all sorts of worried about being judged by everyone else at the table if you share your thoughts.*
>
> *Action: You silence yourself and let yet another opportunity to be heard pass you by.*

So what if your next idea is not the best idea ever - it's *yours*!

If it's something you have to say, then say it. Stop holding it in and watch what happens.

---

## Your Turn

Is *I Shouldn't* Hilda keeping your opinions, thoughts, and ideas bottled up? What will you say when it's your turn?

Guess what. It's your turn. It's always your turn. Speak up.

# You'll Never Live Up to Expectations

Carlo is the creator of "The Spectacular Adventures of Zsazsa Zaturnnah," a Filipino graphic novel released in 2003. He wrote this graphic novel out of love, just to put something out there and indulge his creative juices. Now remember, 2003 is before Facebook and social media were even a thing. But when he released the book, expecting nothing, it became the pre-social media equivalent of viral. His book was listed as one of the top books of the year. Zsazsa quickly became a bestseller in the largest bookstore in the country. Carlo was in demand on radio and television and in newspapers and magazines. The book even found its way into university classrooms and curriculum! About a year later, he was contacted by six movie companies and a major producer of musicals - all seeking the rights.

SIX!

What a shock for Carlo.

He did something out of love and suddenly he gained a gaggle of people wanting to take his work to the next level. And somewhere along the way, people started to call him a genius.

So of course, Hilda showed up.

*gulp*

> Holy crap, I did not expect this little thing I did on the side to be ridiculously successful.
> This success is so much more than I would have envisioned for myself.
> I bet the movie would be just terrible.

Despite his fears, Carlo felt an obligation to deliver some sort of genius, to live up to his hype. He had to appease his new fan base. This took a huge toll on his ego.

> *Thought: Hilda manipulates you into believing your first success was a fluke that cannot be repeated.*
>
> *Feeling: You feel tortured by a terrifying sense of impending doom.*
>
> *Action: You drag your feet on your next big thing, or worse yet, decide it's not even worth trying.*

Hilda tortured him with two of her favorite weapons - expectation setting and ego stroking. She pulled the puppet strings and carefully crafted a cautionary tale of what was expected from an unexpected genius like Carlo. And his fans unintentionally chimed in. Through it all everyone kept asking the obvious question:

What are you going to do next?!

Oh there you are, Hilda.

Carlo's overnight success created a whole level of oh-shit-now-what?!

> *Is this idea good enough?*
> *How will you match the success of the first book?*
> *What if the second book doesn't fly as high as the first one?*
> *Can I pull this off again?*
> *Where do I even start?*
> *Can I live up to expectations?*

Similar to how we talked about J.J. Abrams, Carlo was terrified that he'd never be able to follow up his first success with something equally awesome. I've worked with a lot of people over the years who have experienced success early and thought it was the worst thing ever. Hilda is very cruel and she will crap all over you despite epic success and admiration.

Now is your moment to wow the crowd. It's time to inspire the people. It's time to create something new.

But hear this - this is only her viciousness. It is not real. Hilda wants to keep the Carlos of the world obsessed with how things are going to be received so they cannot actually focus on the task at hand. Instead, we should take a lesson from ZsaZsa Zaturnnah herself. She's far too badass for that.

## Your Turn

Have you experienced some early success along the way that has crippled you from figuring out how to take the next big leap? What are you going to do about it?

# Why Can't You Just Be Grateful?

My own personal Hilda loves to pull in overtime with one particular message she's been telling me for years.

> *When are you going to settle down?*
> *You're never happy, are you?*
> *Other people are perfectly content sitting still.*
> *What's wrong with you?*
> *Why can't you just be grateful for what you have?*
> *You're so selfish!*

Ugh. That word - selfish. It just brings up so much emotion for me. I never wanted to be seen as selfish. I like to think of myself as a very generous person. But the truth is I can be selfish and I'm extremely selfish about my coaching practice, who I invite into my world, and the people I surround myself. I want nothing but quality humans surrounding me. Hilda has a field day with this. This was especially challenging when my wife and I had to make a difficult decision.

## Brooklyn. Sunday brunch date. Dead of winter.

Over coffee and mimosas, my wife Meredyth and I got to talking about how much we love our annual cruises. We started discussing where we want to go next time and why we love our cruises so much. When we dug into why, we came to realize it wasn't the vacation or the food or the beautiful places we get to visit. What makes those trips so special is how instantly rejuvenated we both feel when we can stare off at endless ocean. It's inspiring and romantic and grounding and refreshing and just about the best thing ever.

Then we both got quiet. And pensive. And really, really sad.

It's like simultaneously we both had a massive realization. We spend 51 weeks each year working our asses off so we can enjoy ONE week of endless ocean. WTF? Doesn't that seem incredibly backwards? We had to fix that. Since the ocean is accessible year-round there, we set our sights on southern California, thousands of miles away from everyone we know.

*Thought: Hilda pressures you to explain yourself so nobody perceives you as selfish or ungrateful.*

*Feeling: You feel like a jerk for being selfish and ungrateful.*

*Action: You tell lies to make what you want more palpable to others who probably don't want what you want anyway.*

When we told people about our upcoming move, we were bombarded with one question: why? In response, I felt obligated to rationalize our decision. I blamed Meredyth and her new job because that seemed like a socially acceptable reason to relocate across the country. I would say something like, "Well, my wife has accepted a new job there" or "Meredyth got a dream job that we couldn't pass up." I didn't realize I was doing this, but these reasons were fibs, lies, and other distortions. Meredyth went out and found this job after we decided we wanted to move to SoCal, not before. She found the job because we wanted to move here, not the other way around. But because I was so afraid of being perceived as ungrateful for my life in New York City, I felt the need to explain away my selfishness.

But the real answer to the *why* question was simply . . .

## Just because.

As Meredyth pointed out to me, that was the audacious reason . . . and the truth! We decided we wanted a new and exciting adventure just because. And we didn't owe anyone a more practical or acceptable explanation than that.

My wife is so smart.

The truth is, every time I get the selfishness noise in my head, it's usually because other people are feeling jealous of my choices - and the fact that they choose differently. They've chosen a life and they see it as something they can't possibly have control over. I disagree with that happy nonsense. I believe that we are all able to craft our own destiny, to choose our own choices, to make a lifestyle exactly what we want it to be. And if that makes me selfish, I'm perfectly okay with that.

So Hilda, take a number. I don't need to listen to this shit anymore. I don't need to listen to you human Hildas either. I love you and I hope you love me too. But step off my choices and focus on your own.

## Your Turn

Do you find yourself explaining and justifying your decisions and choices to others? What would happen if you replaced all those explanations with the phrase just because?

# It Must Be Nice

Hilda takes potshots at your confidence every chance she gets. Let's look at one of her favorite catchphrases: it must be nice. This is one she busts out all the time, but she didn't just grab it out of thin air. It often comes from the people who love you the most.

Take my client Diana, for example. A couple years ago, Diana and her fiancé (now hubby) decided to move from New Jersey to Paris. This was a big, exciting, and slightly terrifying move for her. It was so far away from her friends and family and all of her clients, but she always wanted to live abroad and this was her chance. Most people around her were exceptionally supportive and enthusiastic for her. Unfortunately, some others felt the need to not-so-politely insult her decision to move to Paris by saying . . .

*Oh, that's not practical.*
*I could never move so far away from everyone I love.*
*But you don't speak French. How will you do anything?*
*It's just not realistic.*

And, of course, the pièce de résistance . . .

*Gee, it must be nice.*

Ugh.

These Human Hildas were envious of her opportunity to move to Paris, and envy breeds ugliness. On top of that, they don't quite know what to do with their uncertainty and discomfort about someone they know doing something so spectacular, so they put it down. Sometimes unintentionally. Sometimes quite intentionally.

Despite knowing she wanted to move to Paris with all her heart, Hilda amplified their message in Diana's brain. After months of struggling with this strange sort of guilt for chasing her dreams, she finally found a perfect response to this kind of naysaying . . .

## It IS nice, actually. Thanks!

I've never had a client make a big leap who hasn't been slammed with *It must be nice* somewhere along the way.

> *Thought: Hilda insults you for being fortunate.*
>
> *Feeling: You feel guilty for your choices when others don't have and/or don't chase their own dreams.*
>
> *Action: You share less about - even downplay - your successes. You may even enjoy those successes less.*

Hilda hoards these messages just in case you decide to get brazen enough to step beyond your comfort zone. Taking a risk or putting yourself out there? She hits you with a *must be nice* brick, rattling all your mojo and sucking all your juju away.

It all boils down to the fear of appearing selfish. If Hilda has successfully taught you that selfishness is a fate worse than death (which, let's face it, most of society believes) all she has to do is make you feel greedy or self-centered and BAM, she's got you in her claws.

I've got a permission slip for you: want what you want and make it happen. There's no reason to apologize or feel bad about chasing your dreams. While what you want may also affect other people, not chasing your dreams will affect you more. And that's simply not fair. You deserve to be extraordinarily happy, no matter what anyone has to say about it. So there.

## Your Turn

Do you want what you want without apology? Do you chase dreams that others think are impractical or even a little nutty? Then you're doing something right.

This is the definition of *audacity*.

If your goals and dreams come with a side of guilt for being so nice, how could you drop the apology? How can you let others' jealousy be about them instead of you?

# These are the Goals You Should Want

I recently learned that getting on the *New York Times* Bestseller list is just short of a Ponzi scheme. Despite having the reputation of being the preeminent list of the most popular books by consumers every week, the process behind getting on that list is pretty shady. First, it's based on some super-secret method of collecting sales data from "certain vendors" (read: not all bookstores) each and every week. Even if your book were to be one of the biggest selling books of all time, like say *Dante's Inferno*, it won't matter. What matters is the number of books you sell in just ONE WEEK.

Then, apparently when one of the big five publishing houses "sell" a crapload of their latest release to Barnes and Noble, those sales count . . . even though an actual reader hasn't cracked one single book cover open yet. On top of that, these publishers pay big bucks to procure those coveted "New in Nonfiction" and "B&N Bestsellers" shelves to place their authors front and center. And if all that fails, apparently you can buy your way to the top of the list if you've got enough cash.

For authors, this is the equivalent of learning there's no Santa Claus.

This got me thinking about the goals we set, often with little-to-no real understanding of what those accomplishments actually mean. How often do we reach for something simply because society has deemed it "prestigious" or "a true marker of success?"

Take TED and TEDx Talks. There was a time when every coach or author or speaker I knew would sell their first born for the chance to rock that stage, especially the full production of TED. Myself included. It felt like TED was an immense honor that only "discovered" people got the opportunity to do. And since the talks become viral pieces of content, what thought leader wouldn't want to jump at the chance to step into their spotlight?

Professional speaker Frank Swain, for one. In a recent interview, he argues, "I know I'm supposed to swoon a little at the idea of being an Official TEDx Speaker, that doing this will rain down confetti and job offers and fame on me. But in the end it boils down to this: TEDx is just another organization asking me to work for free. I'm tired of the bullshit idea that exposure is somehow its own reward. I'm tired of the people who can afford to do it justifying this malignant trend."

Apparently, there's no Tooth Fairy either.

> *Thought: Hilda tells you what you should want based on what society and/or others value.*
>
> *Feeling: You feel obligated to want these goals and dreams despite not knowing what they really mean or entail.*
>
> *Action: You leave these impossible-sounding goals you didn't even want to begin with on the permanent back burner which makes you feel inferior to others who have achieved such accolades. It's like Hilda's long con.*

So why am I bursting your bubble like this?

One of the slightly backhanded ways that *I Shouldn't* Hilda screws with you is to should you into wanting to achieve certain things because they sound good on paper. These gold stars will make you seem more impressive, so it doesn't really matter if you want these particular gold stars - these are the goals you *should* want. And by making these gold stars seem big and important to you without any real information about what their achievements actually entail, she has you pushing toward Fantasyland.

Take a look at your goals. Make sure you are chasing dreams you truly want for your own reasons, not just because of the impressiveness factor. If that includes the *New York Times* or TED, rock on with your badass self.

And if those goals don't do it for you, rock on with your badass self.

---

## Your Turn

What do you think?

Are you aspiring to something because it's something you've always aspired to? If so, have you done your homework to see what's behind the curtain?

What are you willing to forgo in order to achieve these accolades? Where do you draw the line?

# Why Can't You Be Like So-and-So

Compare = Despair.

I so wish I could take credit for that pithy little phrase, but I did not coin it. It has been a staple in my coaching practice since day one. And despite a good deal of research, I have not been able to figure out who originally said it.

Comparing yourself to others is normal. It's human. It's a way to figure out your place in the world. It's how you see if you're measuring up against the competition. But it's also a slippery slope.

Learning from others is one thing. Ain't nothing wrong with that. Obviously you want to look at people who have successfully done what it is you're trying to do in order to shorten your learning curve. That's just wise. But worrying too much about how others did/do what they did/do is Hilda's way of distracting you from figuring out what you need to do next.

When I started out as an entrepreneur, I thought it would take me one year to become a six-figure coach. That was probably because of the multitude of get-rich-quick-as-a-coach webinars I kept attending. But that's beside the point. So I got a full-time job at The Container Store, selling empty boxes, with the expectation that I would be there for one year, tops - only until my coaching practice exploded.

One year turned into three.

After three years, I went down to part-time at the store. This wasn't good enough for Hilda. All of the entrepreneurs I knew were working full-time in their businesses because "they were serious" - which somehow meant I wasn't.

The truth was I was married and had responsibilities. Many of the entrepreneurs I was comparing myself to were younger and living in their parents' houses building their empires from their childhood bedrooms. That was not an option for me - not because I'm above that, but because my mother died in 1996 and I no longer had a childhood bedroom anywhere in the world. But I was blind to these differences. All I saw was that these other people seemed to be experiencing success at a much greater velocity than I was . . . and I was professionally jealous.

> *Why can't you be more like so-and-so?*
> *He has his shit together.*
> *She's got so much more talent than you.*
> *What's-his-face is bathing in the big bucks. What's your problem?*
> *You need to be more outspoken like all of the other celebrity coaches.*

*I Shouldn't* Hilda loves it when you compare yourself to others. It's a fantastic distraction from doing anything that matters and gets you questioning your worth. It seems ludicrous to me how quickly Hilda can send you spiraling from admiration down into self-loathing in under 10 seconds.

> *Well, she's really inspiring.*
> *I can't wait until I reach those kinds of heights.*
> *It looks like she was where I am just a few short years ago.*
> *It will probably take me twice as long, though.*
> *I wish I was as pretty as she is.*
> *She's really much more confident than I am.*
> *Think I could ever pull that off the way she just did?*
> *Hell no.*
> *She has 25,000 Twitter followers. I don't have a tenth of that.*

*Oh my goodness. I would never even attempt to laugh at myself onstage like that.*
*There's something special about her that I just don't have.*
*Let's face it. I'm never going to be as successful as she is.*
*Wow, I really suck by comparison to her.*
*You know, maybe it's time to rethink this whole direction.*

Obsessing about what somebody else is doing is the fastest way to sabotage yourself. It is critically important that you figure out how to kill all of this comparison thinking, once and for all.

## Keep your eyes on your own paper.

*Thought: Hilda gets in your head so you compare the first chapter in your journey to someone else's seventeenth chapter.*

*Feeling: You feel embarrassment and despair at the thought that you don't measure up.*

*Action: You beat yourself up for not moving as fast, if not faster, than all the successful people who came before you.*

Here are some truth bombs for you:

- When you get down to it, your path has absolutely nothing to do with what anyone else is doing.
- Someone else's successes do not take away from your possibilities.
- The pace at which somebody else works is irrelevant to the pace at which you choose to work.
- The circumstances someone else faces are completely different from the ones you face.
- Just because somebody else has had it easier than you, it doesn't mean your path is impossible.
- Just because somebody else has had it harder than you, it doesn't mean your path is less valuable.

It all boils down to this - quit adding meaning to the differences between you and someone else. There really isn't anything in it for you.

## Your Turn

Who do you compare yourself to? How does that comparison game turn into your perceived inferiority? How can you turn it around so you only compare yourself to others for the purpose of inspiring you to step up your game?

# You're Gonna Become a Douchebag

Let's talk about the fear of fame changing you. While most of us aren't technically afraid of success, we do fear what success might bring. One of the ways that the fear of success rears its head is the fear of fame and notoriety making you a douchebag. Have you heard the adage, "It takes 10 years to become an overnight success?" As soon as you can smell or taste that "overnight success" coming up, that's when you start worrying you're on a bridge that's going to take you from here to douchebaggery.

We want to become a big deal within our peer group. And that means that when we become a bigger deal, our peer group changes. We leave some folks behind...we ratchet up the echelon to the next person, to the next level. And as with anything, new level = new devil.

This whole fear of fame screwing us up and making us into someone we're not is really just another form of comparison thinking. For every example of famous jerks, there is a shining counterexample of people unchanged by their fame. But guess who Hilda focuses on? Hilda is able to convince us that douchebaggery is a foregone conclusion, right? In order to become a world-renowned expert, or a bestselling author, or a speaker who commands $10,000 a talk, or a coach who is booked solid, or whatever {fill in the blank}, you actually have to turn into a semi-Kardashian.

This is just more of Hilda's nonsense. It's a judgment game - how we view (and often talk about) others and how we view ourselves. The idea there will be somebody else out there in the world that would ever think that about us in that light is terrifying and upsetting. We lose faith in our abilities not only to succeed but to keep a cool head or calm ego, "Ugh. I am becoming that girl/guy!" And worse yet, what if one of the people we leave behind, someone that doesn't level up at our pace, thinks... "Oh, them? They're a douchebag now. I liked them when . . . but now he/she's bought into their own hype."

As a life coach, it baffles me how common this is in the life coaching industry. We are people who help others live their best lives and yet we can be so competitive, judgmental, and nasty. And let me be clear, I'm saying "we" here because I've been there and I've done that. One of the things Hilda has taught us is how to discern and compare ourselves to others.

> *Thought: Hilda convinces you the success will go to your head and that you'll turn into a total douche. It's a forgone conclusion.*
>
> *Feeling: You become terrified of success and all that might come with it.*
>
> *Action: You cunningly avoid opportunities where you might raise your profile and shoot yourself in the foot.*

This comparison nonsense ain't doing anyone any favors.

Look, there are a lot of things in this world you can control, but you can't control everything. For example, you can control whether or not you choose to act like a douchebag, but you can't control how others are going to perceive you. So you have a choice:

1. Obsess about how your success could open you up to more judgment and possible haters.
2. Or focus on being you, only more successful.

Oh, and one more note: if you have haters, you're doing something right. People who play it safe and behave themselves rarely get haters. But people who are willing to shake the world by its shoulders and do things that matter will occasionally run into people who are uncomfortable - even threatened - by your audacity. So instead of fearing the possibility of haters, embrace it. Choose it. And when you get your first hater, invite me to your Hater Dance Party. In my coaching practice, this is an event worthy of celebration.

---

## Your Turn

How can you stop fearing your own success and all that might accompany it? What song do you want to dance to when you get your first (or next) hater?

# How Embarrassing!

It is very strange how the demented documentary in your brain works. It doesn't really require creativity on Hilda's part. The experiences she decides to help you re-live don't even need to match or pair up in any way with what you're trying to do next.

Say you're about to launch a book. Maybe she'll screen that moment when you got really drunk in college and barfed all over the place. About to meet the parents of your new love interest? She'll remind you of that time when you shot the last free throw and missed it, losing the big game. It doesn't matter that these things happened 20 years ago.

What is it about the fear of embarrassing ourselves that makes it feel as though it's going to be a lethal experience?

If you're afraid of embarrassment, Hilda wants to make that embarrassment a tangible feeling brewing right below the surface at all times. Her demented documentary is her tool of choice.

> *Thought: Hilda sets up a screening of your demented documentary to show a montage of your most embarrassing moments.*
>
> *Feeling: You re-experience all those humiliating moments and all of the emotional scars that came with them.*
>
> *Action: You stop yourself in your tracks, avoiding even the slimmest possibility of falling on your ass again.*

Living a life where you avoid embarrassment at all costs equals a really small life. You'll never speak your mind. You'll never try new things. You'll never dance like a crazy person. You'll never think outside of the box. You'll never be completely you without constantly worrying about what other people (from loved ones to complete strangers) are going to say or think or notice.

When I was in college, one of my professors had us do this obnoxious exercise. Our job was to walk into a full elevator and stay facing the back of the elevator, instead of facing the doors. Because, think about it, it's a very strange little tradition that when you get into an elevator, you move around like the dots on a die. If there's one person, you stand in the middle. If there's two people, you stand on the diagonal, both facing the forward and looking desperately at the lights as they say what floor you're going to. Who wrote these rules? What's it all about?

Imagine you join six people in an elevator. You step in but don't turn around like convention dictates. In fact, you make eye contact with each of the six people in the elevator and smile. What do you feel? If you're like me, you feel uneasy, uncertain and completely embarrassed. It's obvious you're doing some weird radical experiment and you want to explain yourself. Nope. My professor said to keep your lips sealed and don't explain what it is you're doing. Just make eye contact and smile and own the embarrassment.

Even though nothing bad happened, I was mortified when I stepped off the elevator. That experience is still very, very palpable, and Hilda keeps it handy in her "Worst of Jennie" archives.

Some of you are listening to this thinking, "Huh, not my problem. I love to let my freak flag fly." If that's you, go on with your badass self. For the rest of us, what would happen if you let your freak flag fly? In fact, what is on the damn freak flag?

Hilda wants you to stay small because she wants you to not embarrass yourself. I'm going to convince you embarrassing yourself is not the end of the freaking world. If this particular Hildaism is holding you back, maybe it's time for you to hop on the elevator.

The next time Hilda busts out the documentary footage of embarrassments past, make sure she plays it all the way through to the end of those segments. Sure, you can watch yourself fall on your ass and remember that bitterly embarrassing feeling, but also watch what happened when you got up and dusted yourself off. Watch as that embarrassment faded, slowly but surely. Watch how it sucked, but it wasn't the end of the world.

Avoiding embarrassment at all costs is far too safe for us audacious people. You may even see the humor in the moment in hindsight - let's face it, life's embarrassments are eventually hysterical.

Nietzsche (and Kelly Clarkson) are onto something - "That which does not kill us makes us stronger."

That song is in your head now, isn't it? You're welcome.

---

## Your Turn

Why is embarrassment so terrifying for you? How differently would you approach challenges if you didn't concern yourself so much with the fear of potential embarrassment?

# You Should Never Say No

People pleasing. Ugh. Another nasty "Behave yourself" tactic of *I Shouldn't* Hilda is to convince you that you can never say no.

*I Shouldn't* Hilda loves to tell you what you should do just as much as what you shouldn't.

Chris likes to be needed. She likes to be asked for help. She likes to be liked.

You know. She's human.

Chris is a self-proclaimed people-pleasing overcommitter. She has been known within her community as the go-to person you can always count on to chair that committee, run that fundraiser, or launch that initiative. If you ask her for help, she'll never turn you down. Because her Hilda has convinced her that she should never say no. And this makes her particularly susceptible to takers.

Takers are people who zap a helluva lot more out of your life than you realize and leave you exhausted. People in your life (often family members) who tend to take more of your emotional energy than they give back. Takers are exhausting. You know somebody is a taker when your phone rings, you look at the caller ID, you see their name, and you go, "Ehhh...oh crap! I don't want to answer that phone call." If you're anything like me, you usually pick up that phone call as quickly as humanly possible just to get it out of the way and over with, because letting it go to voicemail means you have to listen to the voicemail and call them back. This gives them even more attention somehow.

People pleasers like Chris tend to accommodate more than their fair share of takers, fueling *I Shouldn't* Hilda with loads of her nonsense.

> *You always lend a helping hand. It's who you are.*
> *If you say no, they'll never ask you again. You know that would break your heart.*
> *I wonder what they'll think of you if you refuse to help out.*
> *You can make time to help with another fundraiser.*
> *Nobody else will do it like you do. You might as well do it right the first time.*
> *Who cares if you don't really want to do it? Don't be so selfish.*
> *If you want to keep your friends, you should just say yes.*

With this noise reverberating in her head, whenever a taker asks her to do something, Chris's knee-jerk reaction has always been an immediate "sure!" Then upon reflection, she often feels resentful of overcommitting yet again to something she really didn't want to do in the first place.

## She needed some serious boundaries.

That said, I knew that building and reinforcing boundaries for Chris was going to be challenging after a lifetime of letting people take her for granted. So we co-created a stop-gap measure to kill her sure habit. We decided Chris would simply replace the word "sure" with a new phrase – "hmm, let me think about it and I'll let you know." Now instead of committing immediately in the moment, she had a quick and dirty stall tactic which allows her to take her time and consider the request thoughtfully. Then she can respond based on what she wants to do, instead of emotionally reacting based on what she should do.

By giving herself this breather, saying no is so much easier. She has time to think through the opportunity and decide if there's enough in it for her to justify the time and energy it's going to take. Most of the time, she concludes it's not worth it and politely declines. She now only volunteers for activities she wants to be involved in; she no longer feels volun-told into activities she really doesn't have time for. She is less available, less responsive, and a heck of a lot less apologetic to her takers.

> *Thought: Hilda gets you to believe you should never say no if you want people to like you.*
>
> *Feeling: You feel obligated to commit to anything and everything that's asked of you in order to keep the peace and keep everyone happy.*
>
> *Action: You overcommit to things you don't really want to do and Hilda celebrates that you're now too busy to chase your audacious dreams. Another win for Hilda.*

Do you say yes to far more things than you actually want to be involved in? Take a page from Chris's book and give yourself time to think it through.

And one more note on takers. You're reading this book because Hilda is already doing a number on you, right? She's already sabotaging your best efforts. Why, oh why, oh why would you surround yourself with more takers that are hitting you just like Hilda does? Consider limiting and/or eliminating participating in these relationships. You with me?

## Your Turn

Are you an overcommitter, too? Are you afraid to say no? What stop-gap phrase might you use for the next request to give yourself breathing space to thoughtfully decide whether or not this opportunity is something you want to tackle?

# You SHOULD

We spend enough of our lives trying to walk the freaking tightrope between what we should and shouldn't do. Attempting to please everyone by behaving appropriately and never causing a ruckus is akin to suffocating your audacity.

## *I Shouldn't* is total BS.

So stop letting Hilda feed you *shouldy* thoughts.

Nobody can tell you what you should or should not do.
Nobody can tell you what you should or should not want.
Nobody can tell you what you should or should not attempt.
Nobody can tell you what you should or should not enjoy.

Look. You only get one spin on this big, beautiful, blue marble and it's entirely and solely up to you to make it really count. This is no time to behave. This is no time to worry about what everybody else is doing. This is no time to hold yourself back. So stop *shoulding* all over yourself.

This is the time to grab the world squarely by its shoulders and shake it to its core. Because you are on the brink of something spectacular - I just know it - if you'd only let go of all of this *should* crap.

Be you.

Want more.

Make something spectacular happen.

# CHAPTER FIVE

# BS Belief #3: I Don't Know

Next up, we have *I Don't Know* Hilda. This chick does not want you to cross a starting line—EVER! To keep you in your comfort zone, Hilda calls upon you to rethink, reconsider, and second guess your big ideas. The amount of indecision she stirs up is breathtaking. When this is your predominant Hilda, your knee-jerk response to everything is uncertainty. It's not that you feel incapable or fear making a decision necessarily, it's really that you are afraid of the unknown, the possibility of regret. And you sure as hell do not want to relinquish control.

The reason this is so pernicious is because Hilda has convinced you that it's true!

*You don't know!*
*You can't possibly know!*
*Is that right?*
*There is no right answer, anyway.*
*You can't possibly choose.*
*If you're wrong, which you will be, it will be disastrous.*

Voila! You have not done anything to change the world, because you don't know what's going to happen. You don't know how it's going to look or feel or what you're up against. You don't even know if this is the right starting line for you!

Over thinkers in the house will relate big time to this Hilda. *I Don't Know* Hilda is racked with inertia. She is not willing to make a decision to save her life. Hilda doesn't want you to make a decision because as soon as you do, that means you're going to actually go outside of your comfort zone. That certainly can't be safe! By instilling indecision and inertia, this tricky Hilda makes sure you hang out in the planning phase from now until eternity.

This particular fear of failure is rooted in the idea that "I'll make the wrong choice and fail." Hilda convinces you there's no possible way you could know everything you need to succeed. Thus, you avoid the starting line like the plague. Setting goals feels impossible, and there's nothing worse than someone asking you what you *do* want!

This can quickly spiral into full-on panic. Here's how the second-guessing cycle of suckdom works:

You have an epic idea.
You get insanely excited about this idea.
You share this idea with others. Others share in your excitement.
Hilda shows up with her happy nonsense.
You question your excitement.
You look at your once epic and exciting idea again with unfair scrutiny.
You fall down a rabbit hole of *what ifs*.
You conclude that you were wrong all along. It's just another bad idea.
You have another epic idea . . . but it's clearly bound for the same fate.

Sound familiar?

All at once, that once epic and exciting idea that you were flirting with got sucked into this nasty cycle of second-guessing. Crummy, right?

## Yeah. That crap ends now.

Let's examine how *I Don't Know* Hilda works to keep you stuck in inertia and indecision and explore ways to get beyond this naysaying noise.

# You Know Nothing

. . . Jon Snow. Wait. No. Different book.

In my coaching practice, I enforce one strange but very specific ground rule. You're not allowed to say "I don't know." This includes any fancy variation of the phrase - and I can spot 'em from a mile away.

> *I'm not quite sure.*
> *I'd have to think about that.*
> *Before I answer that, let me ask you . . .*
> *Gee, I've never really thought about that before.*
> *That's a really good question.*
> *That's a really hard question.*
> *That's a really ____ question. (People love to praise my questioning skills in an attempt to not say "I don't know.")*
> *Huh?*

I've heard them all. There's a very specific reason I have decided to insist upon this important ground rule - there is information in your initial response! Even if you change your mind in five minutes, or five days, or five weeks, or five years, there's vital information in what bubbles up right away. We shoot down those thoughts immediately with the elaborate distraction of "I don't know."

Most of us say "I don't know" to the most basic questions every single day. "What do you want for dinner?" seems to be the most common question that elicits this response. Usually it's something like, "I don't know. What do you want?" You're probably reading this and thinking "That's not terribly important, Coach Jennie." And you would be right. Except, if it's difficult for you to say what you want for dinner, how on Earth are you going to answer the bigger questions about what you want?

All of my coaching conversations boil down to three basic questions:

## What do you want?
## Why do you want it?
## What are you going to do about it?

If the answers to any of these questions is "I don't know," then you are not taking responsibility for your own life. But it's not entirely your fault.

> *Thought: "But I really DON'T KNOW!"*
>
> *Feeling: You feel at a total loss when people ask you what you want.*
>
> *Action: You never search your soul for what you want because you're convinced you can't possibly know.*

The phrase "I don't know" is basically as ubiquitous as "um" and "ah" in the English language. We reach for the "I don't know" with so much frequency, we don't even realize it. After years of this, it's difficult to stop. That is until you start working with me. Suddenly you become keenly aware of how often you delay a decision with these three little words.

I think my obsession with killing this phrase came from being a kid in the 80s. Nickelodeon had a television show called "You Can't Do That On Television." For those of you who remember those fantastic days of rainbow suspenders, you know that every time one of the characters said the phrase "I don't know," a bucket of green slime was magically dumped on top of their head. This never failed to earn a laughing fit no matter how many times this shtick was used - and if memory serves, it was used at least once per episode.

I really wish that that existed in the real world. It would break this bad habit with a speedy vengeance.

Over-dependence on this phrase is a sneaky little Hilda method of training you to believe that you do not know what you want, that you do not know why you want things or do things a certain way, and that you don't have a freaking clue what to do next. I call BS on this. It's not that you don't know. It's that you have stopped answering questions when asked. Believe it or not, you're simply out of practice.

---

## Your Turn

It's time to untrain your brain from this knee-jerk response. I want you to raise your awareness to how often you use this annoying little phrase, including fancy IDKs. For bonus points, ask your best friend/spouse/significant other/coworker/accountabilibuddy to perk up their ears and listen for the next time you reach for an "I don't know."

# Are You Sure About That?

We've all heard the old adage, "hindsight is 20/20" - that after you've done something, after you've experienced it, after everything is behind you and you've crossed the finish line, you can look back and see what happened with perfect clarity.

For *I Don't Know* Hilda, this is super scary. Eventually you're going to be able to see what you've done, every mistake you've made, and every misstep with perfect 20/20 clarity. Isn't that what's so debilitating? Isn't that what's so paralyzing? And isn't that what keeps you in indecision in the first place? If you don't make a decision, you can't make a mistake, right? If you don't try, you can't fail. This is what Hilda so compellingly persuades you to believe. Obsessed with your mistakes, she's exceptional at reminding you of any misstep you've ever made. Now, *I Shouldn't* Hilda is equally obsessed with your mistakes, but for different reasons. *I Shouldn't* Hilda is worried about mistakes because they are going to be embarrassing.

*Someone will notice!*
*You're gonna make an ass of yourself.*
*Don't upset anybody around you!*
*You gotta make sure that you make your mom proud!*

*I Don't Know* Hilda is completely different. *I Don't Know* Hilda's fear of failure is that 20/20 vision thing; it's the realization you can't avoid mistakes. Mistakes, in and of themselves, are absolutely, unquestionably unacceptable to *I Don't Know* Hilda. She doesn't want you to ever screw up, because screw-ups are internally humiliating. Screw what other people think - she knows how it will feel! She knows it will hurt. And so, according to Hilda, it's a helluva lot better to be stuck in indecision and second-guessing everything than it is to have done something that you wish you wouldn't have. Bottom line: *I Don't Know* Hilda is terrified of regret!

> *Thought: Before starting something new, Hilda reminds you of a time you made an embarrassing mistake. \*gasp\**
>
> *Feeling: You instantly feel your stomach drop and experience that moment of utter humiliation all over again. That feeling is even amplified for good measure.*
>
> *Action: You backpedal faster than you've ever backpedaled before.*

Hilda insists you can't possibly predict every potential outcome. She preoccupies your thoughts, time, and energy with spinning scenarios and reminders that preparation and planning is pointless. She corners you into wallowing in indecision. Certainty is unattainable. There is no amount of knowing, planning, plotting, or anticipating that can ensure we've thought of it all. We cannot protect ourselves from failing, so Hilda corners us into inertia to protect us from even trying. But nothing great can ever be accomplished if we buy into this BS belief and choose to hide from regret with Hilda by our side.

Reality check: you're never going to be 100% sure because you don't have a crystal ball to predict the future. And that's how it should be. Just because you can't know the future, it doesn't mean you don't have a heck of a lot of power in the situation.

---

## Your Turn

What's underneath all that? Why are we so afraid to say what we want and commit to our choices? And really now, what's the worst that could happen?

# You Don't Know Enough Yet

How do you know when you actually know enough? Is that a destination you're ever going to reach?

A very close cousin to *I Can't* Hilda's "You're not qualified" Hildaism is the nagging claim that you're too wildly under-informed to move forward with something. When Hilda tells you that you don't have the qualifications or the chops to be what you want to be or do what you want to do, she is really attacking who you are as a human. But sometimes, it doesn't really work. Instead she has to directly attack what you want.

This is where you fall down the rabbit hole of what my dear friend and mentor, Karen Graves, calls an addiction to infocrack.

There is an infocrack epidemic happening in the world of solopreneurship. When we become solopreneurs, the first thing we do is become students of all things entrepreneurship.

This is not a bad thing. We all gotta start somewhere.

But let me ask you: how many ebooks and bootcamps and programs and information products on entrepreneurship have you purchased?

Mmhmm. Okay.

And how many of those purchases did you actually crack open and engage with?

Uh huh.

Now, how many have you actually implemented?

Yep. Thought so.

Let's face it. Most of these things end up in a folder on your computer collecting cyber-dust.

> *Thought: Hilda tells you that you need to learn more, much more, before you can proceed.*
>
> *Feeling: You experience the high you get from indulging in more infocrack.*
>
> *Action: You spend the next two weeks reading dozens of sales pages and creating a highly complicated spreadsheet of information products you might buy to teach you all this information that you believe you need to learn in order to get started. You may even buy something and read the first few pages before watching more cat videos on YouTube.*

This stuff is inspiring and motivating and oh-so-easy to buy into. It all starts with the need for more information. But it doesn't stop there. Research mode takes over and you start checking out all of the latest offers from the big name people with the fancy pants websites. Research mode is fun! It's one of Hilda's favorite stall tactics. She will encourage you to stay in research mode for as long as possible. It often looks like this:

*Learning is good for you.*
*And totally socially acceptable.*
*And that offer with the free opt-in was unbelievably sexy and you couldn't miss out.*
*Module 1 is a whole lot of the same old, same old - so just skim it.*
*Dive into module 2, you don't have to actually do the homework.*
*Oh, look! A new program about Facebook ads. That seems much more urgent.*

*You should buy it right after you finish reading Gary V's latest blog post.*

This comes up in my coaching practice with almost every single solopreneur client because of the ever-changing nature of being an online entrepreneur. I also fall victim to infocrack addiction from time to time. What I've come to realize is, with a few exceptions, most of the how-to programs were really purchased by Hilda. Somehow, she convinced me I didn't know enough yet, somebody else knows better than I do, and this next how-to program has the secrets of the Universe that I just cannot figure out by myself.

It's a tricky little line to know whether or not this is true or if Hilda is lying to you. In my case, it's true that I didn't know jack about Facebook ads. It's a lie that I needed to take a course on crafting the perfect coaching question. The way that I know if it's a truth or a lie is what I did with the actual information. I followed through on the Facebook ad stuff. The other program I gave up 40 pages in.

Learning a new tactic or a slightly different spin on something is just so much more fun and easy then implementing what you already know.

And, it's not just programs. It's YouTube videos and podcast series and books (clearly I'm not talking about this book) and webinars and workshops and conferences and other learning modalities. All can keep you in second-guessing research mode instead of jumping over the freaking starting line. I am willing to bet you have all the knowledge you could possibly need already inside you.

Enough already! Stop buying new programs and downloading new opt-ins. Implement all you've already learned from the dusty ones. You know more than you think you do.

You're a grown person. You don't need sugar with your medicine. It's time to implement!

---

## Your Turn

Open up that dusty cyber-file of yours. The one that's filled with the latest and greatest infocrack from all the gurus. Delete half of them. Identify the one most likely to contain the information you actually need right now, crack it open, and implement, implement, implement.

# Not Yet, But As Soon As . . .

At some point or another, we all fall prey to putting off our dreams until everything is perfect. I know I've been there. Have you?

Here are some common examples:

*I will write my book as soon as I have more time.*
*I will consider changing careers as soon as I have more money saved.*
*I will start dating as soon as I lose these last annoying pounds.*

Now I ask you: has *as soon as* ever actually arrived? I mean, how do we know that we're actually "ready" to leap?

We have become masters at delaying our dreams by inventing what psychologists call displacement activities. I like to call this phenomenon *busy procrastination.* It's a slightly more sophisticated form of putting stuff off by purposely busying yourself with something that "seems" like a step in the right direction, but in reality is just an elaborate stall tactic. Here are some busy procrastination examples I've heard from coaching clients:

Instead of working on any of my dusty resolutions for this year, I'm spending time announcing new ones for next year so I can start fresh, come January.

Instead of completing a task on my endless to-do list, I'm going to continue researching and testing the latest task list apps and productivity systems until I find one I like.

Instead of eating a healthy lunch, in keeping with my weight loss goal, I'm going to hit the fast food drive-thru. I know I'm going to overindulge during the holidays anyway so it makes no sense to take care of myself now. Besidesm if I gain a little weight this month, I'll have a higher starting weight in January and more to lose, which will mean an even better accomplishment next year.

Yes, I'm sassing up these stories a bit and paraphrasing to illustrate their absurdity, but not much. You are busying yourself with sorta-tasks that make you feel like you're making progress, but you're fooling yourself. What you're really doing is searching for motivation instead of doing what you know needs to happen.

Unreadiness is a common affliction, even among the most ambitious dreamers. Instead of furiously taking bold action, it's easy to fall into a pattern of waiting until you've done more research, trying to understand everything, and/or getting approval from others before taking the next step.

Here's the hard truth:

In order to be extraordinary, you must break through the illusion that your dreams exist somewhere out there, outside of your reach, after everything else is *just so*. You can't wait for everything to be checked off your to-do list before you start creating a life you love. If you do, you will perpetually live in "as soon as" land.

It's time to get off your ass, people! Just GO! Now is all you have. It is better to take the leap and learn while in action than to sit around and only launch when it feels perfect - which often never happens. Take a giant step forward today – even if you don't feel ready. Just go for it. Do your best with what you have now. You can always perfect it later!

The past can pester you, but it's behind you. The future may have that spooky "unknown" vibe, but you're heading to it no matter what.

You only have this lifetime to make your mark.

> *Thought: Hilda reminds you of something less important you could be doing, thereby distracting you from that more important task. She's sneaky that way.*
>
> *Feeling: You feel productive and safe since you're doing the less scary, more comfy task.*
>
> *Action: You run out of time to do the more important things, but your dishes are done. At least you're getting something accomplished, right?*

Do you have the pluck to believe that you have something important and significant to contribute to the world? (Because you do.)

Do you have the nerve to believe that any less than extraordinary is unacceptable? (Because that's true.)

Get into action. Make it work as you go.

The age of *as soon as* has ended. TODAY you begin.

---

## Your Turn

What are your *as soon as* statements? What are your displacement activities? What would happen if you stopped waiting and just got started today?

*"You can't be that kid standing at the top of the waterslide, overthinking it.*
*You have to go down the chute."*

~ Tina Fey

# But What If . . .

Too many people waste a crapload of time and energy feeling crappy about their past. You carry around buckets of regret and self-loathing everywhere you go. You dwell on your shortcomings, on what your life lacks, on what you don't have and don't get from others. In a nutshell, you are constantly looking backwards.

One of my coaching clients, RJ, is a big fan of *what if* questions. As an expert in productivity and technology, she relies on her natural curiosity and *what if* questions to diagnose problems and arrive at solutions in her work. These questions come from a place of wonder. This is a strength.

Unfortunately, because she's wired to reach for a *what if* when she is working with a client, she has a tendency to fall deep down a rabbit hole of worrisome *what-iffing* when puzzling out a challenge for herself.

> *I think this is a great idea, but what if I'm wrong?*
> *Or what if I try to get my idea off the ground and learn that someone else has already done something really similar?*
> *What if they did it better than me?*
> *What if I don't really have what it takes to pull this off?*
> *What if I devote all this time and energy to starting this project and then I get bored?*
> *And what if there's another idea I've not even thought up yet that's better?*
> *Yeah. What then?*

Oof. Notice how all that *what-iffing* gets spun into a web of a LOT of Hildaisms really quick?

*What-iffing* is an elaborate *I Don't Know* Hilda tactic. It's self-sabotage by way of worry. You are laying the groundwork for mayhem and expecting failure. If Hilda can keep you worried and problem-focused, you'll never see potential solutions.

> *Thought: Hilda has you asking yourself a litany of what-ifs about a new possibility.*
>
> *Feeling: You're confused and worried and obsessing about all the possible negative consequences that could come your way.*
>
> *Action: You overanalyze the possibility until it dies a slow and lonely death.*

The best way to call BS on a *what if* question is to answer it. Hilda wants us to ask *what if,* and then feel the emotions that revolve around it: the fears, the anxieties, the nervousness, the "holy crap, that could possibly happen!" stuff. If we answer the questions, and say "Well, what if it happens? What would I do about it?" it usually takes the wind out of her sails.

So every time Hilda sticks one of the problem-focused/worry *what if* questions in your path, ask a solution-seeking/wonder question immediately after.

> *I think this is a great idea . . . and what if I'm right?*
> *I wonder who else has already done something similar so that I can learn from and/or build off of their work.*
> *What if I can do it differently somehow? Even better?*
> *What if I actually pull this off? What would that look like?*
> *I wonder what will happen next once I pour more time and energy into this project.*
> *I wonder what else I'm going to learn or discover along the way.*
> *I can't wait to see where this goes.*

## Your Turn

What are your *what-ifs?* Are they problem-focused or solution-seeking? What if you dropped all the worry and embraced the wonder? What might come of that?

# You Can't Choose

So let's talk about being weird. Like I mentioned earlier in the book, we humans tend to simultaneously strive to fit in and stand out. We all have our quirks, our oddities, our uncommon opinions, and bits of our lifestyles that go against the grain . . . and Hilda hates that about us.

When you make choices in life that are the antithesis of what's expected, different from how you were raised, or in any way bold and unsettling to the people who love you the most, Hilda gets you all riled up over the chance of making the wrong choice.

So you question yourself. And your decisions. And your choices. And your priorities. And your convictions. And even your sanity. Is this dream unconventional and revolutionary? Or is there actually something wrong with you for wanting this in the first place? It's the existential hokey pokey.

The most common example I've seen in my coaching practice is women who don't want to have children - ever - but battle Hilda's guilt trips for years. (As one of those women myself, this one cuts deep.)

*I know you say you don't want children now, but you don't really know that.*
*You'll regret not having kids someday.*
*All women have a maternal instinct, even if they don't know it yet.*
*Who will take care of you when you're old and senile?*
*Don't you like kids?*
*Your mother really wants you to have kids before she dies so she can play with her grandchildren.*

*The woman gave you life. The least you could do is give her grandchildren.*
*What kind of monster doesn't want to have children?*

Most childfree-by-choice women I've met wrestle with Hilda for years on this even though they know in their bones they've chosen the right path for them. The same goes for any unconventional, impractical, illogical, or straight-up odd choice made in life.

The nagging thoughts and fear of regret can disempower you entirely and make you second guess your convictions, no matter how deliberate and deep-seeded they may be. Sadly, many people concede to this particular flavor of *I Don't Know* Hilda because the self-doubt, second-guessing, and internal turmoil is far too much to bear.

> *Thought: Hilda manipulates you until you don't know your own mind.*
>
> *Feeling: You feel isolated and weird for wanting something unconventional.*
>
> *Action: You fail to choose.*

Here's a quick reality check: this is your life. Yours. No one else's. Your current situation is the result of all the choices you've made up until now. They may not have been the right choices, they may not have been the wrong choices . . . but they were *your* choices. This Hilda's job is to stop you dead in your tracks and make sure you stop choosing. Remember, she's trying to keep you safe.

## But your failure to choose is actually a bold choice. It's the choice to not succeed.

Trust your gut. Choose what's right for you whether or not it's logical, whether or not it's practical, whether or not it's conventional or expected. Whether it's right or wrong . . . choose.

And own your choices! Normal be damned.

---

## Your Turn

How does your fear of regret keep you in a holding pattern? Would you choose differently if you could let that go? What would you choose?

# No Pressure, It's Only Life or Death

Megan is in the process of becoming a foster parent - a process, for her, that's slathered in copious amounts of "unknowns" and "never-befores." There are lots of hoops of fire to walk through, including something called a home study, where a social worker comes into your home, assesses you and your home, and then makes a relatively subjective judgment about your ability to be a good foster parent.

As the day of her first home study visit with the social worker approached, her brain went into overdrive with a long list of things she needed to do to get her house in order and make the perfect first impression.

Make your bed.
Vacuum the floors.
Clean the bathrooms.
Empty the dishwasher.
Buy new sheets for your bed.
Iron the duvet cover so it's not all wrinkly.
Polish the linoleum in the kitchen so it's nice + shiny.
Tear apart, sort, purge, and reorganize all of your closets.
Sweep and wash down the 4'x6' concrete slab you call a patio.
Shop Amazon for hours to find a great couch cover to hide that tear.
Identify all your books with questionable titles and replace them with some bibles, and figure out what the hell crumpets are, make some by hand, and serve them with tea, and knit an afghan that screams PLEASE PICK ME for the arm chair you'll force the social worker to sit in . . .

Okay, so I may have exaggerated a little bit toward the end of the list. But not by much!

In a coaching session two days before the scheduled visit, Megan was completely paralyzed by overwhelm. Because the stakes were so high and her heart is so deeply invested in this, her original goal of getting her house in order and making a good impression turned into a frantic and dramatic fiasco.

The end goal was no longer to put her best foot forward at the visit. No. Her end goal became survival. Hilda was popping up with all sorts of reminders of how she couldn't just be her best self; she had to be the best ever in order to overcome her perceived flaws. Or. Else. She. Wouldn't. Ever. Become. A. Foster. Parent. EVER.

{cue dramatic horror flick doom music}

> *You're already behind the 8-ball being single and childless - you HAVE to make up for that.*
> *If this worker doesn't approve of you, you'll never fulfill this dream + you'll be heartbroken for all of eternity.*
> *You'll fail this home study and have to live with the fact that you didn't do enough to prepare.*
> *You're going to let everyone down if you screw this up with your messy house.*
> *You have ONE SHOT, Megan . . . one chance to do everything right. Your entire future hangs in the balance here, lady.*
> *You will end up homeless, penniless, and everyone you love will shun you.*

I'm really not sure where that last one came from. Boy, did Hilda have a grip around her that day!

As you can tell, this particular Hildaism demonstrates *I Don't Know* Hilda's penchant for the dramatic when the stakes are high. Similar to *what-iffing*, but to the extreme. She shows up with her suitcase full of life-or-death Hildaisms when certain desired outcomes lie outside of our control.

*Thought: Hilda turns on the drama by blowing the importance of insignificant details completely out of proportion.*

*Feeling: You become paralyzed by overwhelm and terror as you take a ride on this emotional rollercoaster.*

*Action: You participate in your own crazy reality show where everything seems extreme.*

She'll pour a bucket of gasoline on your discomfort and lack of control, strike a match, and light up your fears in a blaze of Hilda glory. It's super dramatic. But it's a relatively simple fire to douse.

When facing a goal like this that feels so exceptionally big, it's essential to have people around you who will snap you back into reality and put out the Hilda blaze. In Megan's case, she picked me to dole out one of my signature cathartic shoves and work with her to put Hilda in her place.

As important as the next big thing may be, it's just the NEXT big thing. It's not the ONLY big thing you'll ever do/achieve/create/etc. If it fails, you'll bounce back and figure out what to do next. If it succeeds, you'll celebrate and figure out what to do next. You just need to cross one starting line at a time.

And in case you're curious, Megan only tackled tasks 1-4 on her list, which was more than sufficient. Her home study visit could not have gone better and the social worker didn't notice the tear on the couch.

Take THAT, Hilda.

## Your Turn

Do you relate to these feelings? All that emotional drama that you're bringing to the table is not freaking necessary. Get a grip on reality. Again, this task is not the end all, be all. Find your person (or people) who will lovingly and not-so-politely tell you to shut up and keep going.

And whenever possible, be that person for others.

*"You tried your best, and you failed miserably.
The lesson is, 'never try.'"*

*~ Matt Groening*

# Someday

Sara is consistently superb at keeping her commitments. She over delivers on virtually all of the commitments she makes to her friends, family, boss, or coworkers. In fact, she is probably the most reliable person I've ever met.

But with the commitments she makes to herself? Uh, that's a horse of a different color.

She makes appointments with herself but moves them.

She thinks about her strategy for hours on end, but gets distracted before implementing it.

She sets aside time for her own creative work at the beginning of the week, but then never makes the time for it because life gets in the way.

She's not sure she's ready to spring into action, so she's researching a new methodology first.

Now I know Sara is fully committed to her creative pursuits, but whenever I push her to prioritize her most important work, she tends to talk about it with tentative language.

> *I might...*
> *I was thinking that perhaps . . .*
> *But I'm fixin' to...*
> *I've been considering . . .*
> *I hope to be able to...*
> *Pretty soon, I think I'm going to....*
> *I mean, I'm going to try . . .*

*You know, someday.*

Yeah. Not. Good. Enough.

I call this maybe-perhaps-someday-might-soon language "hedging." It's like hedging your bets - you're not actually taking the full risk because you are only sort of committed. I think Hilda teaches you to talk about your commitments in this way in order to build in a "get out of jail free" card. With these hedging preambles in place, you've given yourself an out before you've even started. I mean, you tried, right?

Didn't Yoda teach you anything? Sheesh.

This tentative language isn't just weak word choices; it's a sign that you are half-assing your dreams.

> *Thought: Hilda trains you to speak with tentative, hedging language about what you want.*
>
> *Feeling: You feel uncertain and wishy-washy at best about your most important endeavors.*
>
> *Action: You make half-ass commitments and let yourself off the hook repeatedly.*

When you hedge about your commitments to yourself, you are planning to fail. You can quote me on that.

Stop hedging! Commit. Set deadlines. Leap. Go all in.

Give yourself the same level of respect and reliability you give everyone else around you. You deserve nothing less.

# Someday ain't on the calendar, people.

Warning: Now that you've learned about hedging, you'll catch yourself doing it all of the time. You'll also notice when people around you hedge.

I'm sorry . . . and you're welcome.

---

## Your Turn

What are your go-to hedging phrases and statements? How will you catch yourself the next time you use this hedging language?

Raise your awareness to how often you speak in this manner. This awareness is half the battle. Start a tally or a coin jar for whenever you catch yourself hedging and make a freaking commitment instead.

# What About These Other Things?

*I Don't Know* Hilda likes to act like the world is on fire. She convinces you that there's no possible way you can get started on the next big thing because there are far too many way more important, urgent, vital things that you need to do first. And just like her nasty habit of sniffing that infocrack, she's exceptionally good at making it difficult to discern the difference between truth and fiction.

What could possibly be more important than leading your life in the way that you want to? Than living audaciously?

Not a damn thing.

Now this particular Hildaism works for both avoiding the starting line (*I Don't Know*) and avoiding the finish line (as we'll discuss later in *I Don't Wanna*), but in my experience, the former is much more common.

> *Thought: Hilda convinces you everything is uber-important and urgent.*
>
> *Feeling: You feel overwhelmed and obligated to tackle everything.*
>
> *Action: You try to be superwoman (or superman) by prioritizing all of the things and actually accomplishing very little.*

Hilda wants to convince you that EVERYTHING is essential. She may even trick you into a little martyrdom thinking with "if you don't do it, it won't get done right." Newsflash: this is total BS designed to keep you from starting what's really important.

Greg McKeown's fabulous book *Essentialism: The Disciplined Pursuit of Less* taught me something about prioritization I never knew.

> "*What is new is how especially damaging this myth is today, in a time when choice and expectations have increased exponentially. It results in stressed people trying to cram yet more activities into their already over-scheduled lives. It creates corporate environments that talk about work/life balance but still expect their employees to be on their smart phones 24/7/365. It leads to staff meetings where as many as ten "top priorities" are discussed with no sense of irony at all.*
>
> *The word "priority" came into the English language in the 1400s. It was singular. It meant the very first or prior thing. It stayed singular for the next five hundred years. Only in the 1900s did we pluralize the term and start talking about priorities. Illogically, we reasoned that by changing the word we could bend reality. Somehow we would now be able to have multiple "first" things. People and companies routinely try to do just that. One leader told me of his experience in a company that talked of "Pri-1, Pri-2, Pri-3, Pri-4, and Pri-5." This gave the impression of many things being the priority, but actually meant nothing was.*"

(I told you that we self-help authors have to define terms. It's a rule. We don't question it.)

We have to, as my boy McKeown puts it, develop "a disciplined pursuit of less but better." Choosing to devote your time and love and attention solely to the essentials requires you to delegate, delete, and otherwise avoid the rest - aka the nonessentials.

---

## Your Turn

Take off your cape, superwoman. You don't need to be everything to everybody. Even if you could do it all, you can't do it all well. So choose the few essential things that you actually WANT to do and ditch the rest.

Prioritize.

Prioritize.

Prioritize.

# You're Not Ready

If you're anything like the dozens of audacious people I've coached before, you've experienced a *This Shit Just Got Real* moment.

I've had my fair share. Choosing your goals and dreams is the fun part, right? You're all crazy inspired, ready to chart a path, and eager to get started. Right on!

Then, panic sets in. Your projects suddenly feel hard and just shy of terrifying. *I Don't Know* Hilda gets to work . . .

> *OMG are you really going to do this?*
> *You just told everybody we know and you can't let them down.*
> *Maybe you didn't think this through all the way.*
> *How the @#%& will you be able to accomplish all this madness?*

Sound about right? Don't worry. I've got you.

This not only means that you're thinking about doing something that matters, it means that you're truly committed to getting it done. You decided to step into your audacity. You've answered all the *what-ifs* and made decisions. Perhaps you've shared them publicly. Deep down you're completely committed to jumping over that starting line and beelining for the finish.

*deep breath*

That pause can be the most exciting or the most terrifying moment when leaning into something that is exhilarating. It is Hilda's last stand; her last hope of conquering and forcing you into the *I Don't Know* headspace. She's going for a "fight or flight" reaction here by jolting your body with a blast of fears in ways that would put a defibrillator to shame.

Your job is to recognize that your *This Shit Just Got Real* moment has arrived, take a big breath, and then cross the freaking starting line. Once you cross the starting line you have passed the point of no return. This is happening now, come hell or high water. You want this. Charge ahead!

> *Thought: Hilda concedes this might actually happen and then inserts a jolt of terror.*
>
> *Feeling: You completely lose your cool and freak out.*
>
> *Action: You are now faced with a fight or flight moment. If you're audacious, the choice is obvious.*

Not only do I want you to embrace and celebrate when you have a *This Shit Just Got Real* moment, I want you to seek them out. To truly lead a big, juicy, unapologetic life, you must shake the world by the shoulders, challenge yourself consistently, and leapfrog from one *This Shit Just Got Real* moment to the next.

Imagine a world full of people who are no longer riddled with inertia and indecision, who instead actively strive for *This Shit Just Got Real* moments. It would definitely be world changing.

---

## Your Turn

When is the last time you experienced a *This Shit Just Got Real* moment? When will it be the next time?

# You KNOW

I get it. Crossing the starting line of your next big thing is super scary. Sure, it's exciting, but it's also terrifying. This is important to you. So you don't want to cross over the point of no return before you know without a doubt that you're ready.

And you could still learn more.

And there's a whole host of possible scenarios you could consider.

And you can't ever be 100% sure.

Uh, that's life, my friend. Hate to break it to you, but someone has to.

Look. This *I Don't Know* noise is total BS. You know enough. You will figure it out as you go.

You're just participating in Hilda's tap dance as a way to stay on this side of the starting line and stay comfortable a little bit longer. I understand. In fact, I'll give you another moment to second guess yourself.

{imagine Coach Jennie humming "The Girl from Ipanema" here}

Okay. About done? Because it's time to get your ass across that starting line. You have far too much to offer the world to stay stuck in indecision and inertia another moment. You know it's time. You know you can handle it. You know I'm right.

Consider this your cathartic shove from inertia to momentum. Start!

# CHAPTER SIX

# BS Belief #4: I Don't Wanna

Finally, we've got *I Don't Wanna* Hilda. *I Don't Wanna* Hilda is not so concerned about starting things. In fact, most people who have a strong *I Don't Wanna* Hilda start stuff all the time! They love the starting line! They cross it like it's nothing. Finishing is a whole other story. As soon as they can smell the paint on the finish line, they start freaking out. They start dragging their feet. They start sabotaging EVERYTHING! Believe it or not, second-guessing shows up over here, too! They start questioning their process. They start overcomplicating things—adding unnecessary steps while displacing true priorities. Hildas who are obsessed with *I Don't Wanna* are stubborn, frustrated and love to insist that things are just too hard.

Finally, *I Don't Wanna* Hilda convinces you to put off your badassery by artfully and skillfully justifying procrastination. Just filling your head with the phrase *I Don't Wanna* convinces you that you need motivation in order to accomplish anything. When your strategy is to wait for motivation to magically show up without being prompted, your productivity is in big trouble. Sure, when you are feeling motivated, your strategy will seem to work swimmingly. But unfortunately, whenever you don't really feel particularly motivated, that very same strategy sinks your battleship and sabotages your progress. Since your feelings change without notice, choosing motivation as a strategy sets you up for almost certain failure.

Of course, Hilda also keeps this motivation at bay by distracting you with time-sucks and trivialities. She's quite evil like that.

*I Don't Wanna* Hilda can seem like the nicest of the mean girls until you see beneath her shallow Hildaisms. She likes to incite your self-sabotage by complimenting you or encouraging you to let a deadline slide. She might commiserate with you when you're feeling tired or bored. She'll urge you to wait until you feel inspired or to sit still until all the right conditions are magically in place. She'll distract you with shiny objects, help you come up with an awesome excuse, or remind you that you're super special.

Don't be fooled. She's a wolf in sheep's clothing. She's just like the quintessential *Mean Girl*, Regina George, telling you that your bracelet is really pretty to your face, then telling others how ugly it is when you're out of earshot, all the while plotting your demise. Know better than to believe her twisted, two-faced lies.

In this section, we're going to point out the devious ways that *I Don't Wanna* Hilda holds you back and how to beat her at her own game. Dive right in; don't put it off.

# But You Don't Feel Like It

Picture this.

After checking your email on your iPhone for any emergencies, you finally decide to crawl out of bed and start the day. While the coffee pot steams and sputters, you open up your laptop, bracing yourself for another day in the life of the grind. You pour yourself that first cup, make a massive sigh of disgust, and begrudgingly sit down.

For one reason or another, you are just not feeling "it" this morning. Perhaps if you check your email again, something in there will motivate you to get to work. You delete two or three junk emails, reply to another quickly, and mark all the other client messages as new so you can respond to them later - when you're fully caffeinated. Then, you promise yourself you'll come back to the dozen or so newsletters that need reading. Surely there is information inside that you absolutely need. But later. Not now. It's just too early.

Email feels overwhelming, so you move over to Facebook. Much more fun! You post a few comments here and there until you stumble upon a genius quote that inspires you. It's so good you just have to share it. But what to do with it? Should you share it on your personal Facebook timeline? Maybe create a graphic for Pinterest? Ooh yes! And then put the graphic on Instagram and then link it to Facebook and Twitter? Yeah.

Dammit. Coffee got cold. Time for a refill.

Okay. It's been almost an hour since you got out of bed and you're still not feeling motivated. After beating yourself up for what you haven't done yet, you finally bust out your to-do list and ask yourself a seriously dangerous question: what do I feel like doing?

> *Thought: Hilda hides all the motivation in a closet somewhere and distracts you with shiny objects.*
>
> *Feeling: You feel bored or tired or otherwise unmotivated and uninspired.*
>
> *Action: You do absolutely nothing. Because without motivation you're justifiably unable to be productive. Perhaps you'll join Hilda for bonbons today.*

If the scenario above resonates for you, then you are probably using motivation as your go-to productivity strategy – and it's the worst strategy imaginable. You hope some external pressure (read: motivation) will come along and prod you into action. Let's set the record straight right from the get-go . . . Motivation is a crock. While it does feel good, motivation is completely unreliable. It relies on your emotions and your emotions are constantly changing. You simply do not have the luxury of waiting! You need to get things done - immediately if not sooner!

Tenacity is a much sounder strategy. Instead of hoping the right emotions are going to line up at the right time and place, tenacity is something you can muster immediately. You simply decide you're just gonna do it because you said so. Emotions be damned.

I know you may be surprised that, as a life coach, I insist motivation is a heap of BS - but allow me to prove it. I personally guarantee that choosing tenacity will feel different. In fact, it might not feel like anything resembling motivation or inspiration. It's gonna feel like accomplishment . . . which can in turn make you feel motivated. Funny how that works, eh?

Accomplishing things is the best way to inspire yourself. Tomorrow, as you're winding down your day, try writing your daily Ta-Da! list instead of focusing on your endless To-do list. Celebrate what you actually got done and watch what happens.

## Your Turn

Accountability is the perfect partner for tenacity!

Add some serious accountability into your life by drawing on the strengths and support of others. This may mean hiring a business coach, joining a mastermind group, working with an accountabilibuddy, or a combination of the three. More than just personal cheerleaders, accountability partners are there to track your progress, keep you inspired, and ensure that you don't quit. Perhaps you don't need a whole team of people – like mine – and just one person will do. Everyone could use someone to push them along towards their short-term goals.

Let go of your need for motivation and choose to do something that propels you forward today – starting right this minute – whether you feel like it or not.

# But It's Not Perfect Yet

Today, I'm coming out of the closet!

(deep breath)

I'm going to share with you one of my biggest challenges as a human being - my fear of imperfection! Yep, that's right. The Audacity Coach herself is so afraid of imperfection that she struggles to finish anything.

There. I said it.

(another deep breath)

You'd think that a life coach would know better and be able to get over this crap. You'd think that because I have expertise in organization, productivity, and prioritization that I would be able to muster the discipline to get things done. But like most overachievers I know, I want everything I do to shine like the top of the Chrysler Building. It's not that I think I'm perfect - far from it. It's that I let Hilda fill my head with perfectionist pleas so often that I keep myself from finishing new and exciting projects.

Oh, and do I have a crap load of unfinished projects! There are dozens of half-written articles and oodles of not-quite-completed workbooks. I also have several personal projects of mine that reside permanently on the backburner. I'm surrounded by somewhere-between-started-and-finished projects that rarely come to fruition.

And I know I'm not the only one. We perfectionists get caught in a nasty cycle I like to refer to as a perfectionism loop:

Start a project . . . *revved up and raring to go*
Brainstorm and outline ideas . . . *still enthusiastic*
Start putting together the big pieces . . . *enthusiasm begins to wane*
Start seeing how impossible it is that the project will turn out perfect
. . . *start losing steam*
Pick at the project without making any significant progress . . . *self-loathing sets in*
Move on to new project . . . *utterly deflated by another unfinished project*

Sound familiar?

> *Thought: Hilda demands nothing less than perfection.*
>
> *Feeling: You experience the despair of imperfection followed by some self-loathing.*
>
> *Action: You quit, yet again, and become utterly deflated by another failure.*

Perfectionism is just a convenient excuse for procrastination. Hilda loves our perfectionist tendencies. If perfection is your goal and perfection is unattainable, you'll never finish anything. If you never finish anything, Hilda gets more of those celebratory bonbons she loves so much.

Instead of striving for perfection, reach for the finish line. Adopt the mantra *Better Done Than Perfect*. It's better to meet your goals imperfectly than failing by default because you've chosen to chase the myth of perfection.

## Your Turn

Which of your projects is stuck in a perfectionism loop? What would you be able to finish if you adopted the mantra, *Better Done Than Perfect* for yourself?

# You Just Can't Today

Achievement requires follow-through. Seems straightforward enough, right? Designing dreams and goals is the easy part. You discover a passion that truly drives you. You get excited, chart a path, and get started. Woohoo!

But then, something fizzles. While you honestly know in your heart that this is right for you and exactly what you want, at some point you stop going after it with the same fervor you started with.

WTF?

*I Don't Wanna* Hilda is an eager accomplice in these moments. She encourages the self-sabotage by placating and validating your lack of inspiration:

> *You just can't today.*
> *If you're not feeling it, you're not feeling it.*
> *It's okay.*
> *You can try again tomorrow.*
> *Wanna see what's on Netflix?*

> *Thought: Hilda hints that you don't have to do anything today if you don't want to.*
>
> *Feeling: You feel lazy yet validated and convince yourself you'll do something about it tomorrow.*
>
> *Action: You accept Hilda's endless supply of procrastination permission slips and binge watch another show on Netflix.*

If this sounds like you, you're not alone. Many of my clients struggle with follow-through. The feeling of accomplishment when you've completed one small task on time is fantastic and addictive. On the flipside, when progress stalls it feels just like failure. This feeling then often leads to even more stalling - or abandonment of your goals all together! Been there? It sucks!

When you find yourself stalling, there is always a reason (read: excuse). Ask yourself the following questions:

Did I give up?
Get turned off by all the hard work?
Decide I no longer need it?
Think I no longer deserve it?
Change my mind about what I want?
Discover a new passion or priority?
Adjust my goal to meet new criteria?

Sometimes you just don't feel like it. I get it. There were days when I was putting together this book when I just didn't feel like it. This is normal and human and happens to the best of us. But, if you want something, go get it! Don't let *I Don't Wanna* Hilda convince you to give up so easily.

---

## Your Turn

Become emotionally connected to your goals! See them as your babies - you'd never abandon your babies. Follow-through is simply a natural part of the process. Set a bold but realistic action plan for achieving your goals.

Then set yourself up for success – daily, weekly, monthly, and ultimately. Be consistent. Need help with all that? Get a follow-through partner to hold you accountable. If need be, hire a coach to encourage you along the way.

# It's All or Nothing

Melissa came to me when she found herself deep in the throes of a quarter-life crisis. She had never really asked herself what she wanted. Rather, she simply went after the things she knew she could handle with the very least amount of effort possible. While her life was easy, it was also boring and uninspired. She was pretty good at her job, but hated her boss and loathed going to work. She was unhappy with her health and fitness levels, referring to herself repeatedly as "a rooted couch potato." She lived in an apartment she could barely afford with her boyfriend so she could "look impressive and entertain a lot," while relying heavily on credit cards. She didn't like most of her "crazy high maintenance friends," but was terrified of being lonely, so she stayed intimately involved in their drama. Her only hobbies were watching bad reality television, eating fast food, and complaining about her life to anyone who would listen. Melissa was depressed all the time because she had no direction.

Through our coaching sessions, Melissa discovered a whole new outlook on life and set out to develop the best possible version of herself. She set goals, seriously audacious ones, in every area of her life, including: drop 50 pounds, run a half marathon, find a new job, get completely out of debt, downsize apartments, ditch the toxic friendships, improve her relationship with her boyfriend, stop complaining, go to graduate school, start a blog, write a book, travel to amazing places, learn to design and make her own clothes, and on and on and on! You get the idea. So she decided to dive face first into action and started working on all the goals at the same time. It doesn't take a rocket scientist to guess what happened next...

Can you relate?

After determining a series of big ass goals like Melissa's, you find yourself at the peak of your motivation. You are ready and raring to dive into everything, working furiously toward many goals, across many areas of your lives. While I gotta applaud the audacity of jumping into action and taking on the world, this pace can actually work against you. It's easy to become frustrated and overwhelmed by all the work involved. If you're scattered across a bunch of goals, you can only give a small amount of time and attention to each goal - resulting in only incremental improvements that feel way too slow. Soon, motivation wanes and you give up altogether.

> *Thought: Hilda puts a lot of all-or-nothing thinking in your head.*
>
> *Feeling: You become obsessed with doing everything at once, which becomes overwhelming and exhausting fast.*
>
> *Action: You lose momentum and give up on everything instead of taking one leap at a time.*

It totally makes sense to want to just dive in. You finally have a list of goals - and you want it all YESTERDAY! But it took a long time to build the life you have now; don't you think it might take some time to rebuild this new one, too? Rome wasn't built in a day, my friends.

So, here's my suggestion for anyone looking to completely rebuild their life from the ground up: work in phases! Approach your goals in a way that they will naturally build on each other.

In Melissa's case, "Phase 1" was focused on improving her relationships. She dumped the emotionally draining friends, improved her communication with her boss, opened up about her financial concerns with her boyfriend, and got more comfortable with her time alone. This afforded her the wins she needed to go onto the second phase of her plan. Her focused approach continues today and she's realizing her dreams faster than she ever thought possible. When the going gets tough, she reminds herself that "this is just a phase" and smiles.

---

## Your Turn

Start your first phase with the goals that will strengthen your ability to address the others - your foundation, if you will. Identify some early wins that will give you confidence to get started on the next goal. Then define your subsequent phases, and build on up! Phasing will allow you to spend your energy more efficiently, capitalize on your own successes, and carefully craft a masterpiece of a life that will make your heart sing.

# It's Not Gonna Work for You

*I Don't Wanna* Hilda can be really conniving. Sometimes, she even comes at you with seemingly positive reinforcement! Meet my best friend, Annie. Annie decided she was going to start a new way of eating, but a few days in, *I Don't Wanna* Hilda started chiming in with some strange messages.

See, if she can't convince you of just how unspecial you are with self-doubt (*I Can't*) and self-consciousness (*I Shouldn't*), then perhaps she can get you to quit by backhanded, false flattery.

> *Thought: Hilda makes you believe you are terribly special, a freak of nature even, so this can never work for you.*
>
> *Feeling: You instantly feel defeated and deflated.*
>
> *Action: You give up far too early because you buy into her BS.*

She couldn't convince Annie that she was unable to commit to the plan or shouldn't want to lose weight, but she was able to convince her that she sucks because she is special. There's something super unique about Annie that means she's going to fail. It doesn't matter that this way of eating is founded on hardcore science, and it doesn't matter that it works for so many hundreds of other people (including her own husband!). Nope. According to Hilda, Annie is a complete rarity.

She hurled an odd combination of insults and compliments at Annie.

> *You are a beautiful, albeit fat, snowflake.*
> *You will defy science, and nature, and all the statistics because let's face it, you are an outlier.*

*You are the freak incident.*
*You're just that darn special.*
*You're going to be one of those 2% of people you read about that*
*cannot make this work.*
*What does WebMD think?*
*Your body just processes calories different from every other human*
*being ever.*
*You will definitely fail.*
*It's not your fault, but it is hopeless.*
*Here, have a pie.*

Through sheer tenacity and oodles of social support, Annie has been able to stick to the plan (with very few cheats!). But even after a 10-pound loss, Annie's Hilda (a Jillian Michaels type drill sergeant), still screams at her from time to time.

Thankfully, most of the time, the results speak louder than Hilda's BS.

The key to shutting up *I Don't Wanna* Hilda - even when she's swatting at you with niceties - is to recognize that you are special and you're just like everybody else, too. That means there's just no reason your success story can't come true like it did for what's-her-face and so-and-so.

---

## Your Turn

Does your Hilda ever convince you that your specialness precludes you from succeeding like others? What comebacks do you need when she's attacking you with this false flattery? What sort of results would silence her?

# Life Got in the Way

If I had a nickel for every time I heard the "life got in the way" excuse, I wouldn't have to work another day in my life. This is the catch-all excuse for why people don't meet their commitments - especially their commitments to themselves. I want to hunt down the originator of this particular excuse and give him/her a piece of my mind.

Now, I'm not a monster. I concede that yes, there are times life takes a crap on you and seriously impedes your ability to get things done.

A sick kid.
A car accident.
A chronic illness.
A death in the family.

There are very real circumstances beyond your control that will get in the way of what you want to do.

But these are NOT the sorts of things that I'm referring to here.

It's time to raise your awareness to Hilda's current list of convenient excuses and the day-to-day time sucks Hilda loves to throw at you to slow you down and distract you.

Most of the people I work with are honest, hardworking, committed people who consistently meet their responsibilities to others through tenacious action. They nobly commit themselves in the service of others and are proud of themselves when they make promises and follow through. Sadly, many of these same people readily admit that they do not always give the same courtesy to themselves. Why don't they give themselves the same level of respect?

> *Thought: Hilda excuses you from all responsibility because life got in the way.*
>
> *Feeling: You feel indignant and justified in using this catch-all excuse because you had no control over the situation.*
>
> *Action: You procrastinate or quit altogether. Hilda takes a victory lap around the park.*

Making a commitment to yourself is the key to achieving your dreams - and it doesn't require any selfishness. However, putting yourself first does demand you follow through on your commitments to yourself with the same level of accountability you give to others. It doesn't involve shirking your responsibilities to others. In fact, making yourself your priority is really a loving act to those around you.

This may take practice at first. Make just one small change each day. Be patient with yourself. You'll be surprised by what you will achieve simply by focusing your energy inward.

## Your Turn

Take the following bold actions to make yourself a top priority: Eliminate or delegate unnecessary tasks from your to-do list. Add "No" to your vocabulary, avoiding new commitments that will distract you from your new priority. Set aside daily time and space to work on your goals – and follow through! Schedule some fun time into your routine. And take good care of your physical needs (sleep, exercise, nutrition).

# It's Just Too Damn Hard

Jennifer admits she thought living her dream was supposed to be easy and obstacle-free. She believed there had to be one correct, ideal path for her and all she had to do was keep choosing correctly. She just had to believe and she would attract what she most wants. It would be easy. And magical. Just turn on the cosmic Google Maps to your dreams and follow your gut. Turn right. Left. Left. Correct. Then she'll arrive at her ultimate, perfect life.

At least that's what all the woo-woo gurus taught her to believe.

Unfortunately, when Jennifer experienced a challenge or a misstep, her hypothetical Life Goals GPS did not recalculate her route and take her on her happy way. Her thoughts weren't all, *Oh, let's see where this course is gonna take me* or *Oh, I'm gonna just go back and do it another way.* Hilda took over with thoughts like *what's wrong with you?* And you just wasted so much time. Because the fantasy of Easy Street never manifested like it was supposed to, Jennifer beat herself up.

In the past decade, a lot of credence has been given to the somewhat spiritual idea that if you ask for what you want and visualize it with fervor, the universe will conspire to make it manifest for you - aka the Law of Attraction.

So by this thinking, all you have to do is put your order in at the cosmic success drive-thru, and then just pull up to the next window. What a concept! Let's test it out.

Step outside of your home/office/wherever you are right now. Now see 100 people throwing $100 bills towards you, with smiles on their faces.

Nothing yet? No?
How 'bout now? You want fries with that?

And to poke even more holes in this floofy-mumbo-jumbo, what does manifest even really mean?

*Manifest (v): to make evident or certain by showing or displaying.*

Not "to make something appear because you want it real bad." I have no idea who decided to change the meaning of that word, but I have several bones to pick with them.

Look, positive thinking is plenty powerful. Visualizing your dreams is a great exercise. By all means, see yourself on a stage receiving a standing ovation. See yourself rockin' out your business. See yourself with everything you want. Then, put in the legwork and make it happen.

My point is: you're cute, but the universe isn't exactly on the edge of its seat to hand you whatever you want, just because you asked nicely.

Ok. Stepping off my soapbox now. Back to Jennifer's frustration.

Audacious people do spectacular things. Jennifer came to realize that things are sometimes challenging. In fact, sometimes they are really freaking hard. Sometimes you make decisions that end up sucking. You screw up. You get hurt. You lose money. Sometimes obstacles pop up when you least expect them. Sometimes you realize that had you gone in another direction, it's quite likely that you would have been happier. That's reality.

# It's what you do with that truth that matters.

This reality check freed her up to drive forward without relying so much on magical thinking and without all the self-flagellation.

> *Thought: Hilda fools you into believing this journey is supposed to be magical and easy - otherwise, it's the wrong path.*
>
> *Feeling: You get very sad and frustrated that you're not manifesting like you're supposed to.*
>
> *Action: You beat yourself up, because obviously it must be your fault that this isn't as easy as the gurus promised it would be.*

Look. I like to make fun of the Law of Attraction because it's not my jam. If you buy into the Law of Attraction, don't be insulted. It may surprise you to learn that most of my clients are believers, too. But they don't let their *I Don't Wanna* Hilda have a conniption fit whenever they aren't attracting what they want with ease and magic.

Successful people work. Hard. Relentlessly. Tenaciously.

When it's easy and feels magical, they are grateful.

But when it's not, they don't bitch and moan.

And most importantly, they never ever quit.

---

## Your Turn

Do your most exciting goals and projects often get derailed because they proved harder and less magical to achieve than expected? When that happens, what does Hilda try to do with that information? How can you cut her off at the pass?

# There's Something Wrong with You

Monique recently returned from speaking at a social media conference. She rocked the stage and made lots of connections, but came home exhausted and unmotivated. She reached out to me frustrated that she couldn't get herself back into the swing of things:

"So, I'm fighting with my time management again. I didn't give myself enough time to get stuff done while I was away and I've really fallen behind on my client work. I also have so much follow up from the conference to do. And my inbox is overflowing and that's stressing me out. And I just know I am not going to meet this deadline I have later this week. It seems like self-sabotage to set deadlines that are way too early, yet sometimes it's the right thing to do because it helps me get started. And . . . "

I interrupted . . . "Okay. First, what is on your to-do list today that hasn't been done?"

*"I have to get caught up on my email."*

"Second . . . what time are you working until this evening?"

*"I will probably work from now until 6:00 or 6:30."*

"Okay. Do you have a glass of water? Are you hungry?"

*"I've got coffee and water both. And just ate about three hours ago."*

"Excellent! Let's use the Pomodoro Technique. Okay. I'm starting a timer. I want you to spend the next 25 minutes tackling your inbox. Respond to as many of those emails as you can within 25 minutes with the next step and report back to me in 25 minutes. Race the clock. Ready? Go!"

Now I know Monique was hoping I would dive into a long diatribe about why she was procrastinating and offer an analysis of what's behind her self-sabotaging ways. And I could do that. But that would just be giving Hilda an alley-oop in continuing the procrastination. In other words, she and her Hilda were looking for some commiseration on how tough it was going to be to get back to work . . . and perhaps a permission slip to push the deadline back.

Not on my watch.

> *Thought: Hilda distracts you with a concern over why you are procrastinating again.*
>
> *Feeling: You become angry with yourself - again - for letting yourself down - again.*
>
> *Action: You spend more time procrastinating because now you're in the throes of beating yourself up again. Hilda enjoys popcorn while watching you perform your own version of Fight Club.*

So you procrastinated. Yet again. What's next on the agenda? It's time to curl up in a ball on the sofa and feel bad about yourself, right? Or perhaps you can call someone and analyze why you procrastinate for a couple hours, yeah?

## That's exactly what Hilda wants you to do.

WRONG! Beating yourself up about what you didn't do is the biggest waste of time imaginable. So is overanalyzing why you're procrastinating.

We all do it. I get it. It feels bad when we sabotage ourselves and we want to wallow in this shitty, shitty feeling. But spending time feeling really crappy about what you didn't do is just stupid. Really. What's in it for you to do this?

This is yet another blatant procrastination tactic . . . completely unproductive.

Enough with the naval-gazing on why you're procrastinating. Just do something about it. Immediately, if not sooner.

## Your Turn

From now on, when you catch yourself beating yourself into a pulp for what you didn't do, I want you to train yourself to think the following and then fill in the rest . . .

Oh wait. I'm beating myself up again. Well, that's not productive. What am I gonna do about it?

# Just Quit While You're Ahead

Earlier this year, I sought out Laura and Veronica Childs, authors of *Low Carb High Fat No Hunger Diet & Cookbook*, for help with adopting their way of eating and tackling my food demons. I was terrified. You see, I have been through just about every type of dieting support you can imagine. I went to Weight Watchers meetings on and off for half a dozen years, suffered through nasty Jenny Craig meals for as long as I could stand it (which wasn't long), and I even went to a therapist for quite a while who told me that my weight loss goals were hopeless and I should just give up and get bariatric surgery. Basically, every "official" weight-loss authority I have talked to one-on-one has made me feel fatter and grosser than the last. Every time I've reached out and asked for help, it's backfired spectacularly.

And yet, I decided to consult a nutritionist so I could change my relationship with food and find a sane way to get healthier. I was also looking for a bold way to lose some of the weight that I have picked up as a full-time, work-from-home solopreneur.

At our first meeting, Veronica and Laura assigned a homework assignment much like the ones I dole out to my Audacity Coaching clients. For the next two weeks, they wanted me to eliminate all starches in order to get to the bottom of what was going on in my body. As someone who thinks that pasta should have its very own annual parade because it's so damn tasty, the idea of not eating any starches was mildly anxiety producing. And my brain instantly leapt to Hilda.

*There is no way on Earth you'll be able to do this.*
*If you don't eat starches, what in the world will you eat?*

*You know this is going to be a big fat failure. Just like all other times.*
*Why are you wasting everybody's time?*
*Quit while you're ahead.*

But Laura threw down another challenge, as if to taunt Hilda. She challenged me with a game. I was to text her a picture of everything I ate - before I put it in my mouth. When I made my breakfast, I texted her a picture. If I ate a slice of cheese, I texted her a picture. If I poured myself a glass of wine, that's right, another picture. It was an epic cathartic shove to the woman who doles out cathartic shoves for a living. The pictures kept me honest. And to my amazement, my photographic food journal is turning my meal choices into increasingly Instagram-worthy plates of food. My cooking skills are improving and I'm falling in love with taking care of myself. Who knew?!

*Thought: Hilda grabs that documentary again and screens all of your past weight loss failures.*

*Feeling: You revisit the pain, embarrassment, and hunger while replaying every reel in your head.*

*Action: You arrive at the conclusion that this time will be like all the others and decide to quit before you have to experience any of those emotions again . . . which in turn makes you feel like a quitter. Well played, Hilda. Well played.*

This gamification of improving my nutrition has proven to be absolutely life changing. It's no longer such a freaking chore to eat better; it's surprisingly fun. It isn't hard. It's actually quite enjoyable so I don't want to quit. Imagine that!

Best of all, Hilda is all out of naysaying comebacks on the subject. Don't you love it when you can render Hilda speechless?

## Your Turn

What are you working on that feels like a chore? How might you change things up and turn this journey into a game? Hilda has a lot less power when we're having fun.

# But You've Got a Great Excuse!

Let's have a little talk about excuses.

*I Don't Wanna* Hilda's absolute favorite pastime is dreaming up yet another glorious excuse to add to your growing collection. She turns excuse-making into a freakin' art form, I tell ya.

I've been collecting the good, the bad, and the are-you-even-serious-right-now excuses from everyone and everywhere within my reach for quite some time. From this accumulation of excuses extraordinaire, I've confirmed two things:

1. Everyone, even the most ambitious and focused, makes excuses for not doing what drives them toward their goals.
2. No matter how good they sound in your head, they almost always sound ridiculous if you recite them aloud.

Here I share with you a shamefully long list of excuses that I, my clients, my friends, my family, my community, and even some complete strangers have confessed to using when they didn't want to follow through on something important.

> *But I don't know how to make it happen.*
> *But I'm really tired from my long day. I work real hard, y'know?*
> *I've been working on it in my spare time, but my kids make it so I never have spare time.*
> *There's no way I can take a paycut. I'm only open to change if I can simultaneously maintain my six-figure lifestyle right out the gate.*
> *No one will get me.*
> *It's too hard / too much work.*
> *I'm not perfectly clear on this so how can I share/teach/sell it.*
> *What's the point?*

*Once I have it all planned then I can start.*

*Look! A squirrel! A sale on office supplies! An underoo drawer that needs to be organized!*

*Look at this sink of dishes . . . let me clean this up so I can concentrate.*

*It's not REALLY going to make an impact in the grand scheme of things.*

*But I'll get all sweaty.*

*It's too early/too hot outside/too soon/too raw/too much/too little.*

*Screw it. I'll do it tomorrow.*

*I got stuck in traffic.*

*My boss won't let me.*

*My husband said no.*

*My mom won't like it.*

*My kids, my husband, my mother, father, sister (and I don't even have one), brothers . . . NEED me.*

*If I do what I want, I'll be too busy to take care of what/who's important.*

*I'm being selfish focusing on my needs.*

*I'll be leaving people I care about behind.*

*By the time I get this learned and launched someone else will have monopolized the market . . . why bother?*

*Once I finish this next thing, then I'll be ready.*

*If I do this before she does, her feelings will be hurt.*

*My colors are all wrong for this project. I need a rebrand first.*

*I'm still experimenting with software. When I find the right one, I'll start.*

*Somebody is already doing this . . . and better!*

*No one cares.*

*I'm sure somebody else will make one that will be better than mine anyway so no need for me to make one.*

*You're not that special or original.*

*I don't really know what I'm doing.*

*My kids need me at home.*

*I've waited this long to do \*insert item here\* - no one is going to care if it doesn't get done right now, it can wait.*

*I'm bored with this, I think I'll start working on something new.*

Confession time: how many of these excuses made you wince in agony because you've used them yourself? Do you see yourself in these excuses? Are you sick and tired of holding yourself back by sticking your head in the sand? Are you finally, FINALLY, ready to freaking do something about it?!

If not, why the hell are you reading my book? There are plenty of woo-woo coaches who will coddle you elsewhere. I'm wasting my virtual breath on you and your excuses. Move on.

But if so, YESSSSS! We should talk. Immediately, if not sooner.

No. More. Excuses.

> *Thought: Hilda inserts any and every excuse into your brain on demand.*
>
> *Feeling: You wince in the agony of defeat.*
>
> *Action: You fall victim to that excuse and never finish what you started.*

The number one thing you can do starting right freaking now that will launch your life into the stratosphere is stop making excuses! I know, I know. Sounds simple, unoriginal, and perhaps overly generic. I don't care. I promise it bears repeating!

You learned how to make excuses when your dog started eating your homework and for many of you, you've never stopped. I'm willing to bet that most of you have already made an excuse today. Most of the peeps I work with show up with boatloads of perfectly honed and rehearsed excuses and they are eager to whip 'em out as soon as I start pushing them to the uncomfortable. I don't accept excuses . . . ever!

Your excuses are tired. And very unsexy. You are so much more than that. Start showing it.

When you make excuses, it means you are simply not taking responsibility for your actions. Hear me again, you are not taking responsibility for your actions. Everything you do is a choice. Own up to your choices. Didn't workout today because the day got away from you? Get serious! You didn't choose to workout today. You decided it wasn't important enough to you or that something else was more important (perhaps the television).

Don't want to do something? Okay, then say "I don't want to do that." The most conscientious people make excuses because they really don't want to do something, but they don't want to upset anyone. Don't say, "Well, I can't make it to your event because excuse, excuse, excuse." Say, "no, thank you."

Drop the because. It's either I did this or I didn't do that. Not I did this because . . .

## Stop justifying everything!

When you stop excusing your behaviors and choices, you will be astonished by what comes up. Suddenly, you see your priorities in a whole new light. The people around you will start to take notice of how direct you are and often find a new level of respect for your candidness. Also, the things you've said you've been wanting but not taking action toward suddenly start feeling more possible. You no longer excuse yourself for not gunning for what you really want. So let's see what you got!

# Your Turn

One of the big reasons we make excuses is we are stretched too thin. Stop allowing that! Look at your calendar and to-do lists and start a fresh list of all of your current commitments. Now adjust that list to only commitments you really want in your life. I recommend using the 3Ds - Do it, Delegate it, or Delete it.

Need to get it done yourself - mark the task with Do it and set an aggressive deadline. (No excuses for not following through!)

Not really something that requires your attention but still needs to happen - mark the task with Delegate it, send it over to the appropriate person, and scratch it from your list.

Not really something that needs to be on your plate at all - mark the task with Delete it and move on.

# You WANT This

Once your next big spectacular adventure is underway, Hilda is freaking out. She's pointing out that the finish line is visible on the horizon and there's no knowing what is in store for you once you cross that line. The work part is hard, but the devil you know is better than the devil you don't.

## Yeah. All that *I Don't Wanna* noise is total BS.

Yes, everyone procrastinates. Yes, everyone loses motivation from time to time. This is part of the human condition and beating yourself up about that doesn't help anyone. But now you have the tools you need to shorten the amount of time *I Don't Wanna* Hilda slows you down.

Hilda doesn't want you to succeed. Once you succeed, you're gonna want to tackle more challenges and take more risks. Once you succeed, you're going to feel more tenacious and more confident than ever, and Hilda will lose her grip on your psyche. So she's doing everything in her power to convince you that you don't really want to keep going . . . and that you don't really want this.

There's only one problem . . .

You DO want this.

Look. You don't pick up a book like this - let alone read this far into a book like this - if you're a lightweight. You're sick and tired of being stagnant and are ready to take massive action in your life. You're tired of waiting for your magical thinking to manifest your wish list. You want to activate your inner badass so you can drive your life forward at full throttle. Otherwise, you wouldn't be here.

*"Make it work!"*

*~ Tim Gunn*

# CHAPTER SEVEN

# The Solution

Change your thoughts.

Change your feelings.

Change your actions.

Rinse and repeat.

# For the Next Time Hilda Pipes Up . . .

Remember, fear triggers Hilda. Every time you feel a fear, a particular Hilda response is just a few feet away. You only feel fear when something matters to you. Most of the time when something matters to you, it means you're about to break new ground or break out of your comfort zone or risk something in a big way. Hilda, being the most risk averse human possible, has cultivated a ridiculous number of ways to hold you hostage. And if you don't figure out how to break past all the noise that she's been filling your head with since you were born, you'll never know what you're truly capable of.

The key to making sure your Hilda doesn't keep you from chasing down your outrageous goals is to send her out for coffee so you can confront those fears straight on. And I happen to have some quick-and-dirty steps to help you do just that!

Here's a simple coaching exercise to help you think through — instead of always feeling through — those fears so you can get clear on your next bold steps. Looking at one audacious goal of yours, bust out pen and paper and think through the following:

## 1. What are you really afraid of?

Take a deep breath and just freaking name your fear. Fear of failure, fear of success, fear of the unknown, fear of what others might think, fear of rejection, fear of missing out, fear of change, fear of rocking the boat, fear that you don't know enough, and on and on. I've heard them all (and felt most of them myself!). Breaking down what it really is that's holding you back is honestly 50% of the game.

## 2. Consider the worst possible scenario.

Seriously, go ahead and list all the possible absolutely horrible outcomes that you imagine. You're already thinking about this, so just say it aloud or write it down. Getting real about how bad things could go often gives you a massive reality check — more often than not, the worst case scenario isn't all that bad.

## 3. Imagine the best possible scenario.

Now, list all the potentially great outcomes, you know, if everything goes your way. You've probably not let your imagination run wild in this area yet, so give it a whirl. What kind of awesome is in store for you if you achieve this goal?

## 4. Where in this scenario do you have control?

While you can't control everything, you surely have control over your approach and efforts. List everything you have complete control over. This could include how much you hustle, whether or not you throw in the towel after a setback, how often you put yourself out there, your expectations of others and dozens of other self-controllable actions and inactions.

## 5. Where in this scenario do you have influence?

List where you might not have control, but you certainly have the opportunity to influence how things go down. Depending on your goal, this might look like: how strongly you make your case, how your presentation impacts perception, or how much you buff up on necessary skills.

## 6. Where in this scenario do you have no control?

Some things are just out of your hands. Put that down on paper, too.

## 7. Do something.

Now that you've looked at your fear from all these angles, it's decision time.

You and you alone are responsible for creating your life. And you deserve one that's filled with all the incredible, outrageous and exhilarating things and experiences you want. Yeah, fear is scary. I get that. But so what? Fear ain't got nothin' on you!

Stop feeling your way through this fear thing and put your brain in the driver's seat. Take the time to examine what's really got you stuck, get real with the best and worst possible outcomes, look at the possibilities from every angle, and then, finally, decide for yourself which is going to reign victorious — your fears or your audacity!

This is a bold and perhaps arrogant statement, but I believe it wholeheartedly: Understanding Hilda might just cure cancer.

Seriously. The cure for cancer may be an idea inside someone reading this book. And that idea is just waiting to be unleashed, but is being silenced by an irksome inner naysayer in someone's brain out there. Imagine if that person decides to stop getting sucked into Hilda's BS Beliefs of *I Can't, I Shouldn't, I Don't Know,* and *I Don't Wanna.* What if that person decides it's time to show up?

I hope she does.

# What to Do When Hilda's Right

Let's face it. Sometimes shit doesn't work out. Sometimes no matter how hard you work, how tenacious you are, and how much luck shows up, things don't work out.

This is where Hilda busts out that dreaded video camera to capture your failure experience and adds it to her demented documentary.

## The key here is to not let her get to you.

If you're doing things that matter, sometimes it's not gonna come together like you had hoped. And that sucks. But it's not the end of the world.

The end of the world is when a disappointment or a failed attempt kills your tenacity forever.

# So What?

If you're anything like me, you devour self-help books like this with a hopeful, yet skeptical eye. You're hoping that this is going to be one of those life-changing books that only comes along once or twice a decade, but you're simultaneously reading each chapter with a skeptical outlook wondering whether or not the author is going to answer the most important question . . .

So what?

Now that you've learned all about Hilda, hopefully you're better able to identify when, where, and why your Hilda shows up. More importantly, you're more aware when she does and can more easily differentiate her defeatist nonsense from your truth. And you've armed yourself with techniques to combat Hilda's despicable tactics.

That's great . . . and that's what I hoped you would experience in this book. But again I have to ask . . .

So what?

Now that you've got your hands around your self-sabotaging ways, imagine what could be next for you. Imagine all that potential you've got stored up, out of sight, just waiting to be discovered. Imagine how much audacity you could unleash onto the world if you decided to stop getting in your own way.

So what? So I've taken away all your excuses for not changing the world.

I'm sorry about that. I know how much your self-sabotage protected you from the responsibility of changing the world for the better. I also know how your sabotaging ways gave you something to talk about with your friends. Palling around with Hilda was your hobby. Your pastime. It sucked, but the devil you know is better than the devil you don't, or something like that. And I've ripped all that away from you.

And you're welcome.

You see when I said at the beginning of this book that I am on a mission to instigate audacity in as many humans as possible and then watch the world change, I wasn't kidding.

I've done my part. Now it's your turn.

## So what's it gonna be?

How will you make the most out of your one and only spin on this big, beautiful, blue marble? What can we expect from you?

*Oh Hilda, I get that this scares you . . .*
*but we're doing this.*

*Deal with it.*

# My Letter Back to Hilda

Nice try, Hilda. I gotta admit: it feels like a freaking miracle that I'm holding this book in my hands right now. You did everything in your power to stop me from writing this book. I almost can't believe you didn't win.

You filled my head with doubts and fears and *what-ifs* and *how comes*. I sometimes heeded your defeatist nonsense, wasting time second guessing my next steps or using easy excuses to procrastinate. But you did not derail me.

Admittedly, I did enjoy some of your distractions. I really loved watching all that television with you. Netflix is the best invention since the zipper. And I totally took advantage of all that time you helped me let myself off the hook - it was nice being lazy for a spell. Oh, and the day trips to the beach I took to make myself 'too busy to write'? Those were delightful!

But you couldn't stall me forever.

You made a valiant effort to sabotage me so this book would never see the light of day. You told me *I can't* write a book that will inspire the masses. You told me *I shouldn't* take time away from my coaching practice to chase this dream. You told me *I don't know* enough to contribute in a significant way to the conversation on self-sabotage. You told me *I didn't wanna* take on all that comes with leveling up and becoming an author. But you forgot one thing . . .

I'm stronger than you.

I won. The book is done. And it's pretty damn awesome, if I do say so myself.

Listen, Hilda. I know you worry about me. I know you have good intentions - even though you have a really shitty way of showing you care. I know you'll be here every time I do something that matters to me. I even applaud your consistency.

But I will not let you win. You may temporarily slow me down, but I'm always going to beat you at this game. You really should just give it up.

Please note this in your demented documentary.

# Join the Movement

Thank you again for reading my book. You're part of a movement now – a movement designed to Stop Hilda! Let's make it official. Join the movement and receive your copy of the Handy Dandy Hilda Cheat Sheet and many other surprises.

www.hildathebook.com

# Acknowledgements

(Yep, this part is gonna get me all verklempt. Cue the Kleenex.)

Hilda is the culmination of over two freaking years of my life. And really, even before that, if you count the fact that so much of what I teach comes from lessons I've spent my entire existence learning. But this book would not be possible without the help of some totally amazing people in my life. Gratitude & champagne toasts are in order! Here are the wonderful people I raise my proverbial glass to:

First and foremost, a heartfelt thank you goes to my amazing wife, Meredyth Mustafa-Julock. Your ridiculously generous love and support allows me to do and be and experience everything I've ever dreamed of . . . even when Hilda strikes. I love you more than I can ever tell you. (Oh, and thank you for proofreading the book even when you really didn't have the time. You get lots of points.)

I need to personally thank two insanely tenacious women who helped me develop, package, and deliver this bundle of joy :: the *Book Doula*, Annie P. Ruggles (developmental editor) and the *Book Midwife*, Megan Atkinson (copyeditor and graphic artist). You took my vision for this book, jacked it up about 1000%, and delivered something leagues beyond my imagination. The Hilda movement has been born thanks to you two.

Special thanks to Hilda's incredibly talented illustrator, Renee Bates, who somehow miraculously figured out how to take my descriptions of the Hilda that lives in my brain and turn it into the adorably snide cartoon images seen throughout this book. Hilda turned out perfect – and she knows it.

And I couldn't have pulled this off without the rest of the Audacity Squad: Monique Johnson (video and social media) and Sherree Worrell (project management). What a team!

Much love goes out to my *Auntie Myrna* (aka Uncle Danny) for inspiring me to use the name *Hilda* in the first place. And big hugs to my sisters, Barb Hobart and Debi Vance Skaff, for relentlessly cheering me on from afar - I love you all so darn much.

Thank you to everyone in the Audacity LAB who joined my online events to talk Hilda and help me co-create this beast. Additionally, I have to give special shout-outs of thanks to the following people who have personally helped me along this epic journey in one way or another: Matt and Christopher Roberts, Rebekah Quintana, ChaChanna Simpson, Diana Antholis, Sara Frandina, Chris Laible, RJ Redden, Laura Childs, Joy Dejos, Carlo Vergara, Jennifer Zwiebel, Regina D'Alesio, Kelly Meerbott, Megan DiFeo, Melissa Singer, and many others - but this book is getting really, really long. Oh and a special dose of thanks goes out to my *Book's Baby-Daddy* (aka my mastermind partner) Karen Graves, for loads of inspiration, ideas, and commiseration.

And thanks to all of my Audacity Coaching clients over the years who inspire me every single day. Each of you is extraordinary.

Deep gratitude, hugs, and high-fives!
I love you all!

# Further Reading

Below is a list of the books I mentioned throughout the book and a few others in case you want to learn even more about the topics explored here. If you enjoy devouring books like these, please invite me to your book club.

Brown, Brené. *Rising Strong*. New York City: Spiegel & Grau, 2015.

Carson, Richard David. *Taming Your Gremlin: A Guide to Enjoying Yourself*. New York: Perennial Library, 1986.

Childs, Laura, and Veronica Childs. *Low Carb High Fat No Hunger Diet: Lose Weight With A Ketogenic Hybrid*. CreateSpace Independent Platform, 2d Edition, 2014.

Clance, Pauline Rose. *The Impostor Phenomenon: Overcoming the Fear That Haunts Your Success*. Atlanta, GA: Peachtree, 1985.

Fredrickson, Barbara. *Positivity: Groundbreaking Research Reveals How to Embrace the Hidden Strength of Positive Emotions, Overcome Negativity, and Thrive*. New York: Crown, 2009.

Gilbert, Elizabeth. *Big Magic: Creative Living beyond Fear*. New York: Riverhead, 2015.

Hill, Napoleon. *Think and Grow Rich*. No. Hollywood, CA: Melvin Powers, Wilshire Book, 1966.

Jeffers, Susan J. *Feel the Fear and Do It Anyway*. San Diego: Harcourt Brace Jovanovich, 1987.

Kay, Katty, and Claire Shipman. *The Confidence Code: The Science and Art of Self-assurance - What Women Should Know.* New York City: HarperBusiness/HarperCollins, 2014.

Lyubomirsky, Sonja. *The How of Happiness: A New Approach to Getting the Life You Want.* New York, NY: Penguin, 2007.

Mckeown, Greg. *Essentialism: The Disciplined Pursuit of Less.* New York, NY: Crown Business, 2014.

Seligman, Martin E. P. *Flourish: A Visionary New Understanding of Happiness and Well-being.* New York: Free, 2011.

Sher, Barbara. *I Could Do Anything: If Only I Knew What It Was.* Sydney: Hodder Headline Australia, 1994.

Young, Valerie. *The Secret Thoughts of Successful Women: Why Capable People Suffer from the Impostor Syndrome and How to Thrive in Spite of It.* New York: Crown Business, 2011.

# Hidden Hilda Stories in Film

Cue up Netflix with some of my favorite films and television shows that feature some hidden Hilda stories. Don't forget the popcorn.

*Cinderella.* Dir. Clyde Geronimi, Wilfred Jackson, and Hamilton Luske. Perf. Ilene Woods, James MacDonald, Eleanor Audley. Walt Disney Pictures, 1950. Film.

*Clueless.* Dir. Amy Heckerling. Perf. Alicia Silverstone, Stacey Dash, Et Al. Paramount Pictures, 1995. Film.

*The Color Purple.* Dir. Steven Spielberg. Prod. Kathleen Kennedy, Frank Marshall, and Quincy Jones. By Menno Meyjes. Perf. Danny Glover, Adolph Caesar, Margaret Avery, Oprah Winfrey, Willard Pugh, Whoopi Goldberg, and Akosua Busia. Warner Bros., 1985. Film.

*The Craft.* Dir. Andrew Fleming. Perf. Robin Tunney, Fairuza Balk, Neve Campbell. Columbia Pictures Corporation; Red Wagon Entertainment, 1996. Film.

*Grace & Frankie.* Creators Marta Kauffman, Howard J. Morris. Netflix. 2015

*Heathers.* Dir. Michael Lehmann. Prod. Denise Di Novi and Jon Hutman. By Daniel Waters, Francis Kenny, David Newman, and Norman Hollyn. Perf. Winona Ryder, Christian Slater, Shannen Doherty, Lisanne Falk, Kim Walker, and Penelope Milford. New World Pictures, 1988. Film.

*Inside Out.* Dir. Pete Docter and Ronnie Del Carmen. Perf. Amy Poehler, Bill Hader, Lewis Black, Et Al. Walt Disney Pictures, Pixar Animation Studios, 2015. Film.

*Mean Girls.* Dir. Mark Waters. Perf. Lindsay Lohan, Jonathan Bennett, Rachel McAdams, Et Al. THEVID Technicolor Distribution Services, 2004. Film.

*Muriel's Wedding.* Dir. P.J. Hogan. Perf. Toni Collette, Rachel Griffiths, Bill Hunter. CiBy 2000, Film Victoria, House & Moorhouse Films, 1995. Film.

*Practical Magic.* Dir. Griffin Dunne. Perf. Sandra Bullock, Nicole Kidman, Stockard Channing. Warner Bros., 1998. Film.

*Pretty in Pink.* Dir. Howard Deutch. Perf. Molly Ringwald, Jon Cryer, Harry Dean Stanton. Paramount Pictures, 1986. Film.

*Rudy.* Dir. David Anspaugh. Perf. Sean Astin, Jon Favreau, Ned Beatty. TriStar Pictures, 1993. Film.

*Stepmom.* Dir. Chris Columbus. Perf. Susan Sarandon, Julia Roberts, Ed Harris. Sony Pictures, 1998. Film.

*The Women.* Dir. George Cukor. Perf. Norma Shearer, Joan Crawford, Rosalind Russell. Metro-Goldwyn-Mayer, 1939. Film.

# About the Author

I'm Jennie Mustafa-Julock, The Audacity Coach, but everybody just calls me Coach Jennie.

In case you've not figured it out by now, I don't subscribe to the gentle encouragement coaching thing. My signature cathartic shoves get you unstuck and unstoppable. My BS-free approach to so-much-more-than-life coaching has been the catalyst for my clients to launch new businesses, publish their first books, negotiate career leaps, adventure the world, and more. Simply put, I help driven individuals on the brink of something badass bust through obstacles and build the audacious lives they've been dreaming about. Ready for a Cathartic Shove? Hit me up!

## www.coachjennie.com

Oh, did I mention I'm a professional speaker, too? I'm funny, entertaining, serious when I need to be, and deeply, deeply empathetic to the frustrations of the ambitious, tenacious, and badass! I drink enough of my own Kool-Aid and share my triumphs and failures openly. I'm a gifted storyteller armed with a pile of both moving and hysterical stories to drive my message about Hilda home. Meeting planners, I'm totally the person you need to knock some sass into your audience. Let's talk!

## www.coachjennie.com/speaking

Made in the USA
Charleston, SC
21 January 2017